TURKEY'S POLICY TOWARDS NORTHERN IRAQ:
Problems and Perspectives

Bill Park

ADELPHI PAPER 374

First published May 2005
by **Routledge**
4 Park Square, Milton Park, Abingdon, Oxon, OX14 4RN
for **The International Institute for Strategic Studies**
Arundel House, 13–15 Arundel Street, Temple Place, London, WC2R 3DX
www.iiss.org

Simultaneously published in the USA and Canada
by **Routledge**
270 Madison Ave., New York, NY 10016

Routledge is an imprint of the Taylor & Francis Group

Director John Chipman
Editor Tim Huxley
Manager for Editorial Services Ayse Abdullah
Copy Editor Jill Dobson
Production Jesse Simon
Cover Photograph Getty Images

Typeset by Techset Composition Ltd, Salisbury, Wiltshire
Printed and bound in Great Britain by Bell & Bain Ltd, Thornliebank, Glasgow

British Library Cataloguing in Publication Data
A catalogue record for this book is available from the British Library

Library of Congress Cataloguing in Publication Data

ISBN 0-415-38297-1
ISSN 0567-932X

Contents

Glossary

AKP	Justice and Development Party (Adalet ve Kalkinma)
ANAP	Motherland Party (Anavatan Partisi)
CHP	Republican Peoples' Party (CHP)
CPA	Coalition Provisional Authority
DEP	Democratic Party
IGC	Iraqi Governing Council
IIC	Interim Iraqi Government
ITF	Iraqi Turkmen Front
KADEK	Kurdistan Freedom and Democracy Congress (alternative name for the PKK, April 2002–November 2003)
KDP	Kurdish Democratic Party
KONGRA-GEL	Kurdistan People's Congress (name of PKK since November 2003)
KRG	Kurdish Regional Government
MHP	National Action Party
NSC	National Security Council
OIC	Organisation of Islamic Conference
PKK	Kurdish Workers Party (Partiya Karkari Kurdistan)
PUK	Patriotic Union of Kurdistan
TAL	Transitional Administrative Law
TGS	Turkish General Staff

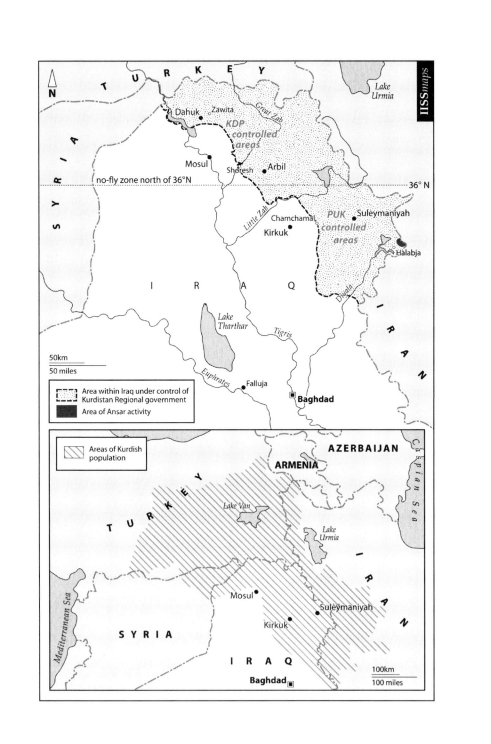

Introduction

In the Iraqi elections of 30 January 2005, Kurds were Iraq's most enthusiastic voters. The Kurdish Democratic Party (KDP)–Patriotic Union of Kurdistan (PUK) list won 25.7% of the vote cast, a figure exceeding the Kurdish proportion of Iraq's total population. This was the second largest vote after the 48.2% share won by the mainly Shi'ite United Iraqi Alliance, and awarded the Kurds 75 seats in the 275-member National Assembly. In oil-rich Tamim governorate, which includes the ethnically mixed and contested city of Kirkuk, the Kurdish alliance won 58.4% of the vote as against the 16% achieved by the Ankara-backed Iraqi Turkmen Front (ITF). The turnout in the Kurdish Regional Government's (KRG) three governorates of Dahuk, Irbil and Suleymaniyah was 89%, 84% and 80% respectively. Tamim enjoyed a 70% turnout. The next highest turnouts were in the predominantly Arab Shi'ite governorates of Najaf (73%), Karbala (73%) and Basra (72%). The lowest turnout, 2%, was in the largely Sunni and desert governorate of Anbar.

These results should boost the Kurds' bargaining power in the deliberations about Iraq's future and, in particular, concerning the future of Kirkuk. In simultaneous elections for the KRG assembly, the KDP and PUK between them picked up over 1.5 million votes of the 1.75m that were cast. An unofficial referendum on Kurdish independence organised by the Kurdistan Referendum Movement was held simultaneously with the national and KRG elections in the Kurdish-populated areas of Iraq; the organisers claimed to have a 98.3% vote in favour of Kurdish independence from the near two million voters said to have participated.[1] This raises questions about how Kurdish bargaining power will be used in Iraq.

On 13 February 2005, the Turkish Ministry of Foreign Affairs released a statement referring to the 'shortcomings, irregularities and infringement of the rules that took place' in the 30 January vote, and singled out Kirkuk in this context. The statement claimed that 'certain elements of Iraqi society attempted to manipulate the voting procedure and extracted illegal gains', and that these shortcomings 'raise serious concerns' about the forthcoming work of the Iraqi Transitional Assembly towards drawing up a permanent constitution.[2] A statement by Turkish Foreign Ministry Spokesman Namik Tan on 28 January 2005 referred to the Iraqi Turkmen's commitment to 'a politically united and territorially integral Iraq', and accused 'certain ethnic groups' (i.e., the Kurds) of 'ethnic and sectarian discrimination' and of 'tabling excessive demands'.[3] In particular, the statement observed that 'the future status of Kirkuk and preservation of its pluralist character' are among the sensitivities that 'have implications beyond Iraq and may undermine regional and international peace and security'.[4] These statements indicate that the elections did not reconcile Ankara to how northern Iraq's political future was unfolding.

The purpose of the 30 January 2005 election was to produce delegates to an Iraqi Transitional National Assembly. A two-thirds majority of the assembly is required to elect a president and three-man presidency, which in turn will appoint a prime minister. The prime minister and council of ministers must have the support of a majority of the assembly members. The main task of the assembly is to draft a constitution by 15 August 2005, which will be submitted to a referendum by 15 October. If the referendum is approved, elections for a new government will be held by 15 December 2005. The two main Kurdish objectives during this process will be to preserve and enhance their autonomy in a federal Iraq, and to extend the Kurdish self-governing zone to incorporate other areas of Iraq traditionally regarded as Kurdish, notably Kirkuk, which the Kurds want as their capital. They will also be seeking to increase the Kurdish ethnic presence in Kirkuk, prior to a referendum that will be held in the city and its surrounding province to determine the ethnic balance there. Ankara's concern will be that Kurdish self-government is as limited as possible and certainly should not approximate full independence, and that Kirkuk remains a multi-ethnic, Iraqi city rather than being embraced by a self-governing Kurdish entity in northern Iraq. Ankara also seeks to maximise the well-being of the Turkmen population of northern Iraq. How uncompromising the Kurds will be in pursuing their objectives, and how far Ankara will go in obstructing and undermining Kurdish progress, will be part of Iraq's evolution throughout and beyond 2005.

Iraq's future is uncertain; consequently, the future of northern Iraq, of Turkish and US policies towards Iraqi Kurdistan and each other, and that of the region as a whole, are also uncertain. Turkey's domestic political development and the internal politics and policies of Iraq's Kurds are two of the key variables, but Middle East and Gulf politics, broader US policies towards the region, Turkey's progress towards EU accession, and transatlantic relations all have a part to play in the evolution of Turkish–Kurdish–US–Iraqi relations. Contained in these complex and dynamic relationships is scope for a range of contrasting outcomes. There are grounds for both pessimism and optimism. This paper explores the background to Turkey's Kurdish perspectives, an account and analysis of more recent developments, and a consideration of some possible futures and the factors that might encourage or thwart their emergence.

Chapter One

Turkey's Kurdish complex

It is largely the Kurdish issue that has ensured Ankara's sometimes reluctant entanglement into the Middle East region's politics. The approximately 30 million Kurds are a largely mountain-dwelling people. Fragmented by tribal, linguistic and religious differences, their ethnic origins and cohesion are obscure and contested, and have in any case become diluted by association with other ethnic groups; nevertheless, the insistence of modern Kurdish nationalism on a common Kurdish ancestry is no less real for all that. Turkey's approximately 15m Kurds make up 20% or more of the country's population and account for about one-half of all Kurds. Iraq's around four and a half million Kurds constitute at least 15% of the total Iraqi population. Iran's Kurdish population is probably a little larger than Iraq's, although a smaller percentage of the national total, and in Syria there are substantially in excess of one million ethnic Kurds.[1] Iraqi Kurdistan[2] is geographically contiguous with the Kurdish-populated areas of Turkey, Iran and Syria. Most Kurds are Sunni Muslims, but there are significant Alevi (a Shia offshoot practiced by mainly Turkish Kurds) and Shia Kurdish populations, and even a Yazidi (an eclectic religion with elements of pagan, Christian, Islamic and older belief systems) minority in Iraq. Until the creation, in the twentieth century, of many of the state borders in the Middle East area, interaction between the largely mountain-dwelling and frequently nomadic Kurds was relatively free and open. It has been said that 'the Kurds only really began to think of themselves as an ethnic community from 1918 onwards'. However, 'for Kurdish nationalists there can be no question that the nation has existed since time immemorial, long asleep but finally aroused'.[3] In other words, the rise of Kurdish national consciousness roughly coincided with the incorporation of Kurds into mostly newly created non-Kurdish states. Partly as a consequence, the twentieth century saw frequent Kurdish revolts against Turkish, Iranian and Arab attempts at nation-building and assimilation.

Given this troubled history, a leading Turkish scholar has explained that 'in Turkish security perceptions, there is no real separation between northern Iraq and southeastern Turkey: they are the geographic and ethno-cultural extension of each other'.[4] The current Turkish Foreign Minister Abdullah Gul has noted that 'for Turkey, the situation in Iraq and the tasks we undertake there are not simply another item on the global agenda. Iraq is our close neighbour, and its future is interlinked with the stability of the region'.[5] The geopolitical significance of recent events in Kurdish-populated northern Iraq is profound for Turkey, more so than for Iran and Syria, because of the size of its own Kurdish population and the two-decades old conflict between the Turkish state and Kurdish separatism in its southeastern provinces. It is also more important than for other European states because Turkey is part of the Middle Eastern regional political system and Iraq is an immediate neighbour. In the run-up to the US-led invasion of Iraq in March 2003, anti-war demonstrators in Turkish cities deployed a pun on the word 'irak' – which in lower case means 'far' in Turkish – chanting, 'onlara irak, bize yakin' ('for them it is far [i.e., irak/Iraq], for us it is next door').

In the eyes of many Turks, Iraq's future, and in particular, that of its Kurds, touches Turkey's core security interests, and even has the potential to threaten the country's territorial integrity. In the Turkish perspective, the Kurdish problem is long term and deep seated. Likewise, this study approaches the Kurdish issue as one with both distant as well as immediate ramifications. Iraq may be on the cusp of a persistent, even deepening crisis that could take years to run its course, with lasting consequences for the stability of the entire region and the territorial integrity of its constituent states. Even a relatively undramatic outcome could have a profound impact on Ankara's relationships with its neighbours, with its North American and European allies, and on Turkish national security. Paradoxically, at the very moment Turkey's European destiny has approached a historic juncture, developments in its immediate neighbourhood, domestic political changes, and US perspectives and interests have combined to reinforce its Middle Eastern destiny. Furthermore, each of these factors is in a state of flux, rendering all consideration of Turkey's future external policy orientation speculative.

Underpinning these observations is more than just a map and a Kurdish population that straddles local borders. There is a psychosis, often referred to as the 'Treaty of Sèvres Complex', that grew out of a 1920 Great Power plan (never realised) to dismember Turkey in the aftermath of the Ottoman Empire's collapse. A feature of this complex is that 'many Turks genuinely believe conspiracy theories in which the US and the EU are trying to weaken Turkey both through partition (e.g., the creation of a Kurdish state) and through instigating sufficient domestic political turmoil to ensure that the country remains weak'.[6] There is also the 'national security syndrome', a term used by former deputy prime minister and leader of the Motherland Party (ANAP) Mesut Yilmaz to refer to the Turkish General Staff's (TGS) 'securitisation' of domestic political issues such as perceived threats from Islamic fundamentalism and Kurdish separatism, and the fusion of these domestic issues with external national security considerations.[7] However exaggerated these elements of Turkish security culture might appear to outsiders, Turkish policy towards the aspirations of both Turkish and Iraqi Kurds cannot be fully appreciated without some awareness of them. An underlying theme of this paper is that in the run-up to the Iraq war in 2003 and since then, US policy has been either insufficiently sensitive towards, or simply oblivious to, the roots and depth of Turkish feeling on the Kurdish issue.

The creation of Iraq; Mosul and the 'Sèvres complex'

Turkey and Iraq are just two of the multitude of states that emerged from the Ottoman Empire that spent decades crumbling away until its final dismantling at the end of the First World War.[8] Strategic considerations and political power rather than ethnographic logic or geographic circumstance account for Turkey and Iraq's mutual borders and those they share with other neighbouring states. These factors also account for the absence of a Kurdish national state. Instead, 'the Kurds found themselves separated from each other by default rather than by design',[9] and were distributed among Turkey, Iraq, Iran and Syria. In the Turkish mindset, and indeed, that of other ruling elites in the region, vigilance is required to ensure no redrawing of the map occurs. Kurdish self-determination is perceived by others in the region and beyond as a threat to the territorial integrity and security of existing states, and to the stability and peace of the region as a whole. There is something to be said for the Kurdish adage, 'the Kurds have no friends but the mountains'.

The slow death of the Ottoman empire under the combined pressures of rising nationalism, more dynamic imperial rivals and internal sclerosis was sealed by its alliance with the losing side in the First World War. Successful revolt against Ottoman rule in the increasingly nationalistic Arab provinces only led to their acquisition by the British and French. By the war's end, the empire had been reduced essentially to its Turkish, Kurdish and Armenian rump, and the victorious allies now agonised over how this rump should be configured. The twelfth of US President Woodrow Wilson's Fourteen Points envisaged 'autonomous development' for the empire's non-Turks, including the Kurds. There was widespread European sympathy for the cause of Christian Armenians, whose territorial claims overlapped those of the Kurds, and considerable British support for Greek aspirations to annex large chunks of Anatolia. The Treaty of Sèvres, drafted by the allies in 1920 to complete the dismantling of the Ottoman Empire, envisaged a substantially expanded Greek presence on the Anatolian mainland, a large Armenian state, European territorial acquisitions in the Aegean and the Mediterranean, and a truncated Turkish state in central Anatolia. The treaty also allowed for a Kurdish state to be carved out of Ottoman territory, should the inhabitants desire it. The former Ottoman and largely Kurdish province of Mosul, a British mandate territory, would be free to join at a later stage.

Notwithstanding this nod towards Kurdish aspirations for self-determination, many Kurdish chiefs fought alongside Kemal Ataturk's Turkish nationalists in the War of Independence (1920–23). To some degree, this can be explained in religious terms, and Ataturk shrewdly cultivated a sense that this was a struggle by the Muslim remnants of the empire against the Christian powers and their local Greek and Armenian allies. Certainly, many Kurds feared that they might find themselves incorporated into an expanded Armenian state favoured by the Great Powers. Nor was the prospect of Arab, or even British, rule necessarily preferable to the establishment of the joint Turkish–Kurdish state that Ataturk was promising. In the event, the Sèvres provisions were swept aside by the Kemalist victory in the autumn of 1922.

The Treaty of Sèvres was superseded by the July 1923 Treaty of Lausanne, to which the newly established Turkish Republic was signatory. No Kurdish or Armenian state was to be carved out of Anatolia. Sherif Hussein of Mecca, who had supported the British against the Turks in return for the promised reversion of Arab-occupied lands to Arab rule, and whose son was in due course to become the first king of the new Iraqi state, had laid claim back in 1915 only to the Ottoman Arab provinces of Baghdad and Basra. The British acquired a mandate over these territories at the end of the war, to which they attached Mosul province. This rendered the generally lower-lying, flat and often desertified Arab-inhabited prov-inces more defensible and economically more viable. Furthermore, oil had recently been discovered around Kirkuk, thus strengthening Britain's desire to incorporate Mosul province into a new Iraqi state over which it could exercise control. Ankara, on the other hand, was determined that the new Turkish state should be made up of the non-Arab Muslim inhabitants of the Ottoman empire, namely, the Turks and the Kurds, and that Mosul province should become part of Turkey. Ankara even proposed in 1923, at Lausanne, that a plebiscite be held to establish the wishes of Mosul's population, which the British refused. Instead, the issue was left to a League of Nations International Commission of Inquiry to investigate, which Ankara believed was bound to favour the British perspective. This is exactly what happened: in a 1925 judgement, Mosul was awarded to Iraq. Turkey protested, but the judgement was deemed binding and, in June 1926, Turkey and Britain signed a bilateral treaty recognising the outcome. Iraq became independent in 1931.

The Kurds were insufficiently united either to ensure the creation of a Kurdish state, or to obstruct this division of Kurdish-populated areas between Iraq and Turkey, and indeed, Syria and Iran. At this stage, Kurdish national identity was barely formed. Kurdish society remained mostly rural, backward, and fragmented linguistically and tribally. Particularly on the lower slopes of the more exclusively Kurdish-populated mountains, Kurds were intermingled with Turkish, Arab, Turkmen, Assyrian, Armenian and other communities. Furthermore, although religion played a large part in Kurdish life, it was not necessarily a unifying factor, and the majority Sunni Kurds were often suspicious of their Alevi kinsmen. From this period onwards and in addition to these pre-existing obstacles to the forging of Kurdish identity, Kurdish unity was further undermined by the incorporation of Kurds into new states created in the wake of the First World War – Turkey, Iraq and Syria – which were all intent on founding identities for themselves.

No Kurdish state had been created, and the small Armenian entity that existed was sealed off by its incorporation into the Soviet Union. The failure to incorporate Mosul province was the new, and large, Turkish state's only loss and could be set against Ataturk's remarkable overturning of designs for a more complete dismemberment of Anatolia. However, although Ataturk's victories are celebrated to this day in Turkey, the predominant legacy of this period is the Sèvres Complex. Anyone familiar with contemporary Turkey will be aware of the frequency with which Turkish officials, journalists and politicians make reference to the Sèvres Complex or exhibit its main features. It is 'a virtual siege mentality',[10] informing Ankara's approach to foreign-policy issues as diverse as Turkey's relations with the EU, its difficulties with Greece in the Aegean, the Cyprus issue and the Armenian 'genocide' question.

Above all, the syndrome goes some way to explaining Turkey's approach to the Kurdish issue. Behind Kurdish cultural aspirations, let alone separatism, and any expression of sympathy with such aspirations, Ankara is inclined to see plans or prospects for Turkey's dismemberment through the lens of the Sèvres Complex. Prime Minister Bulent Ecevit's 1994 declaration that 'the fundamental goal of the United States was to create an autonomous region in southeastern Turkey'[11] represents a still commonplace Turkish assumption and mindset. Ankara's approach to its own Kurdish population, and to developments in Iraq Kurdistan, is conditioned by this sense that Turkey's territorial integrity is insecure and contested, and that the country 'is under continual internal and external threat'.[12]

Furthermore, there are indications that Turkey's grievance at the loss of Mosul has yet to evaporate completely. Thus, in 1986, Ankara reportedly warned the US and Iran that it would demand the return of Mosul and Kirkuk (in effect, the former Ottoman province [*viliyet*] of Mosul) in the event of disorder in Iraq as a consequence of the Iran–Iraq war.[13] During the first US-led war against Iraq in 1991, then Turkish President Turgut Ozal similarly mused about historic Turkish claims to the region in the event of an Iraqi collapse.[14] In May 1995, Turkish President Suleyman Demirel proposed that the Turkish–Iraqi border should be rectified in Turkey's favour,[15] and in December 2003 expressed regret that Turkey had been denied Mosul in 1923.[16] In August 2002, Defence Minister Sabahattin Cakmakoglu, admittedly a member of the far right National Action Party (MHP), chose to remark that Iraqi Kurdistan had been 'forcibly separated' from Turkey at the time of the Republic's foundation in 1923, and that Ankara retained a protective interest in the region.[17] As US-led military action against Iraq became imminent, the foreign minister of the new Justice and Development Party (AKP) government, Yasar Yakis, apparently sought legal clarification of the status of Mosul and Kirkuk,[18] while one of Turkey's leading commentators pointed out that Mosul and Kirkuk were ceded to Iraq, not to any Kurdish state that might subsequently emerge.[19]

Turkey's domestic Kurdish problem

The relationship between the Turkish state and those Kurds who were included in it has been far from happy. Ataturk's early promises that the Kurds would enjoy full cultural and political rights in Turkey were soon broken. Expressions of Kurdish ethnic distinctiveness would not be tolerated. The Lausanne Treaty of 1923 made explicit reference to Turkey's non-Muslim Greek, Armenian and Jewish minorities, but not to its Kurdish and other Muslim ethnic groups. In early 1925, the Kemalist regime embarked upon a brutal repression of a tribal Kurdish rebellion. Although the revolt was initially sparked by the offence given to Kurdish religious sensibilities by Ankara's abolition of the caliphate, a function that had been performed by the Ottoman ruling dynasty, and although most Kurds did not partici- pate, it was evident that the nascent Kurdish identity and resistance to central rule were underlying factors.

The massacres, executions, deportations, incarcerations, destruction of villages and imposition of martial law established a pattern in Ankara's handling of the sporadic Kurdish revolts that occurred throughout the following decades. Ankara had already proscribed the use of the Kurdish language throughout state institutions, including schools, had eliminated all references to Kurdistan in official documents, and had begun the proc- ess of wholesale 'Turkification' of place and personal names. Kurds were officially declared to be 'mountain Turks'. The religious dimension of the Kurdish revolt also contributed to the unleashing of the full force of Kemalism's secularism. Religious orders were banned as the state took control of the teachers, teaching and buildings of Islam in Turkey. Significant Kurdish refugee populations from Turkey were created in neighbouring countries. In a foretaste of Turkey's incursions into Iraq in the 1980s, in 1929 Turkish forces violated the territory of a neighbouring state, in this instance that of Iran, in its pursuit of Kurdish rebels. Before Ataturk's death in 1938, tens of thousands of Kurds had lost their lives, their leadership was decimated, the population dispersed, and the economic infrastructure ruined. Yet revolt and rebellion continued.[20]

Following the foundation of the Turkish Republic, Kurdish revolts in Turkey became commonplace. Before the appearance, in 1978, of the Kurdish Workers Party (PKK), these uprisings were largely spontaneous, tribally based, and generally lacked clearly articulated political objectives. Turkey's Kurds constituted some of the most traditionalist segments of society and inhabited Turkey's least economically developed southeast. The almost incessant round of revolt and repression intensified the social and economic dislocation of Turkey's Kurdish regions still further, and caused many to emigrate both to Kurdish cities such as Diyabikir and to Turkish cities such as Istanbul, today reckoned to contain the largest urban concentration of ethnic Kurds anywhere. Whereas rural southeastern Turkey has become increasingly depopulated, with an estimated 50% or more of Turkey's ethnic Kurds thought be living outside the country's traditionally Kurdish prov- inces, ethnic Kurds make up a significant and expanding portion of Turkey's growing urban poor and working class.[21]

Many of Turkey's leftist intellectuals were also Kurdish, and engaged in the ferocious ideological street wars of the 1970s between the left and the Turkish nationalist right that threatened to tear the country apart. Although these urbanised Kurds were increasingly indistinguishable from their Turkish counterparts, some nevertheless developed a Kurdish identity that was more radical, politicised and articulated than that of the traditional and religiously inclined Kurdish tribal leadership. In 1978, the leftist and conspiratorial PKK emerged from these social, political and demographic transformations. Led by Abdullah Ocalan, in 1984 the PKK embarked on a new and more sustained form of Kurdish resistance to the Turkish state.[22] In what was generally regarded by both sides as a separatist war, Ankara responded with its familiar uncompromising brutality, and a two-decade long war ensued between the PKK and Turkish security forces in which almost 40,000 people have died.[23] This conflict, fought by the security forces with little apparent supervision by politicians, has been associated with the silencing and detention of journalists and political activists, covert assassinations, torture, and scorched earth policies that have emptied around 3,000 Kurdish villages of their inhabitants.[24]

As had happened in earlier phases of Ankara's war against Turkey's own Kurdish population, this new conflict generated a refugee problem. In excess of 10,000 Turkish Kurds fled to Iraq during the 1990s, many of them ending up in a UN-administered camp at Makhmur in northern Iraq, beyond the confines of the self-governing Kurdish Regional Government (KRG) zone. Another 5,000 or so are still believed to be in camps located at Dahuk, within the KRG zone. Although ostensibly willing to accept them back into Turkey, Ankara has been inclined to view them as PKK camp followers. Other Kurdish refugees from Turkey found their way to Iran, Syria, other neighbouring states and, of course, Western Europe, where around 700,000 ethnic Kurds are thought to reside.[25] This diaspora of Turkish Kurds has been at the forefront of the continuing struggle with Ankara for Kurdish self-determination.

Ankara has typically seen its domestic Kurdish difficulties as being in large measure a consequence of external sponsorship of Kurdish separatist and terrorist groups. Of all Turkey's neighbours, the Ba'athist regime of Saddam Hussein's Iraq was seen as the most cooperative and Syria the least with respect to the Kurdish problem. Tired of Syria's sponsorship and protection of the PKK, in autumn 1998, Ankara threatened Damascus with military force unless Ocalan were expelled and the PKK training camps in Syria closed. Damascus complied, and Ocalan's flight led to his 1999 capture, arrest and subsequent incarceration. That Ocalan was under the protection of Greek diplomats at the time of his arrest offered Ankara's hardliners yet more evidence of a widespread international conspiracy against Turkey's strength and security.

Now leaderless and denied its Syrian sanctuary and sustenance, the PKK found that its other sources of external support began to dry up. Improved security cooperation between Ankara and Tehran during the late 1990s reduced Iranian tolerance of the PKK's use of Iranian territory for incursions across the border into Turkey. The Iraqi Kurdish leadership, especially that of the KDP, had for some time resented the PKK's presence and interference in their own fiefdoms, and could appreciate the require-ment to avoid Ankara's wrath. The KDP even fought alongside Turkish security forces against the PKK in northern Iraq. With Abdullah Ocalan imprisoned, the PKK began experiencing internal division and seemed a spent force. In February 2000, it announced a unilateral ceasefire, a gesture that remained largely unreciprocated by Turkish security forces. With up to 75% of its active fighters sheltering in northern Iraq by 1999,[26] it even appeared as if Ankara had finally won its internal war against Kurdish separatism. In 2002, the EU was at last willing to place the PKK on its list of proscribed terrorist organisations.

Turkey's Kurdish war and northern Iraq

At least in the eyes of the Turkish security forces, this success was due in part to its freedom to take the war to the PKK's hideouts in northern Iraq. Until the end of the Iran–Iraq war in 1988, Ankara had an agreement with Baghdad under which Turkish forces could exercise the right of hot pursuit into Iraq. Following Iraq's 1991 defeat in the first Gulf War and the establishment of the Kurdish Regional Government (KRG) in northern Iraq in 1992, the PKK took advantage of regional turmoil to restart the conflict on a new footing. The 1994–98 civil war between Iraq's Kurdish factions – the KDP and the PUK – was also the PKK's most active period in its drawn-out war with Ankara.

However, there was now little to prevent and much to encourage Turkish incursions across the border. In addition to frequent bombing and commando raids, Ankara launched large-scale interventions involving tens of thousands of troops in 1992, 1995, 1996 and 1997. Some of Turkey's Western allies and neighbouring states (particularly Iran) protested strongly against these incursions. Baghdad, too, was increasingly displeased. During the 1997 intervention, conducted largely in support of the KDP in its strug-gle with the (at that time more Tehran-inclined and Damascus-friendly) PUK, up to 50,000 Turkish troops crossed into Iraq and Turkish tanks came within 80km of Kirkuk. These complex machinations and unsentimental alliances show how neighbouring countries can be drawn into the Kurdish conflict and pitted against each other.

Since 1997, Turkey has maintained a permanent troop presence inside Iraq, varying between 1,500 and 10,000 strong. Although the ostensible reason for these military activities has been the need to carry the fight to PKK activists located there, Ankara has meddled in relations between Iraq's Kurdish factions, content to see them at odds with each other, even switching its favours between the KDP and PUK. Northern Iraq had come to resemble a Turkish protectorate of sorts; from 1991 following the defeat of Iraq in the first Gulf War, there is little doubt that Ankara exercised far more influence on events there than did Baghdad. This experience strengthened the Turkish tendency to blur state boundaries in its approach to the Kurdish problem. The US-led war of 2003 against the Baghdad regime shattered these arrangements.

Iraq's Kurds

Developments in Iraqi Kurdistan subsequent to the 1990–91 Gulf War substantially reinforced Turkish sensitivity regarding Kurdish aspirations for self-determination. The failure of the 1991 Kurdish uprising against Saddam was followed by a flood of approximately half a million terrified Iraqi Kurds to a zone near the Turkish border. The resulting humanitarian crisis brought the involvement of a US-led coalition, which created safe havens for the refugees and a 'no-fly-zone' policed from Incirlik air base in Turkey. With the unilateral withdrawal of Baghdad's forces southwards in October 1991, the self-governing KRG zone was established and dominated by the two leading Iraqi Kurdish political parties, the KDP and the PUK. Made up of the three ethnically most Kurdish of Iraq's 18 administrative governorates that nestled up against the Turkish and Iranian borders – Suleymaniya, Erbil and Dahuk – the KRG zone did not extend to the Mosul and Kirkuk oilfields, which form part of what many have traditionally regarded as Iraqi Kurdistan. Despite troubled relations between the KDP and PUK, this experiment in Kurdish self-government has given the inhabitants of the KRG a tangible sense of well-being and freedom.

The KRG zone has thrived economically, relative both to the rest of Iraq and to the period preceding its establishment. This has been partly due to the UN-administered share of income from the now terminated Oil-for-Food Programme that was allocated to the KRG, and partly through smuggling and other illegal and semi-legal activity (now much diminished by the lifting of sanctions against Iraq). Although the KRG has by no means enjoyed a perfect democracy, there has been less of the repression, lawlessness and anarchy that has been the fate of so much of the rest of Iraq since the Kurds broke away. Furthermore, the autonomous period has seen commendable improvements in the region's infrastructure. More to the point, the KRG has afforded its inhabitants a taste of life free from Arab, Turkish or Iranian domination.[27] Arab influence within the KRG area has been substantially reduced. Iraq's Kurds do not lament this.

As Peter Galbraith, former US ambassador to the sovereign Croatian state that had carved its independence from multi-ethnic Yugoslavia, recently described life within the KRG zone, 'the Kurdish region today functions as if it were an independent state. The Kurdistan Regional Government carries out virtually all government functions, and Baghdad law applies only to the extent that the Iraqi Kurdish National Assembly (commonly referred to as the Kurdish Parliament) chooses to apply it. Kurdistan is responsible for its own security (which is the main reason it has been free of the violence wracking the rest of Iraq) and maintains its own armed forces'. He reports 'a widespread antipathy toward Iraq. The Iraqi flag is a hated symbol of a brutal regime, and it is still banned in areas controlled by the Kurdistan Democratic Party (it does fly, along with the Kurdistan flag, on a few public buildings elsewhere in the region). The Kurds do not allow Arab units of the new Iraqi military onto their territory, nor do they permit Baghdad ministries to open offices. They refuse to surrender control of their international borders to Baghdad for fear that the central government will cut off their precious access to the outside world'.[28] They could now hardly be expected to welcome the prospect of a centralised, primarily Arab government controlling them from Baghdad. Ankara, too, finds it implausible that Iraqi Kurds would willingly trade self-government for reintegration into the uncertain enterprise of a post-Saddam Iraq.

Although the KRG's autonomous zone was afforded protection by Ankara's readiness to permit the US and UK to enforce the 'no-fly zone' from Incirlik airbase in Turkey, and despite the fact that Turkish security forces had in effect enjoyed a free hand in their struggle with PKK elements based on the Kurdish-controlled Iraqi side of the mountainous border with Turkey, Ankara never fully acclimatised itself to the existence of the KRG.[29] Before the 2003 war, the situation was tolerable for Ankara because it could intervene freely against the PKK and enjoyed a degree of influence over the main Iraqi Kurdish factions. However, its preference for a revitalisation of Baghdad's authority in the region, whether under Saddam or a suitable successor regime, remained. In the absence of an effective regime in Baghdad, Ankara regarded its own incrementally increasing involvement in northern Iraq as a satisfactory alternative.

What Ankara was not willing to contemplate was the emergence of a truly autonomous Kurdish state in northern Iraq. It feared this could serve as a pole of attraction for Turkey's restive Kurds, or that it might become emboldened enough to lend them direct support. Such a state could garner international sympathy for the idea of wider Kurdish national self-determination, incorporating southeastern Turkey, or might lead, ultimately, to a sovereign Kurdish state. Ankara suspects that full independence and sovereignty is the ultimate goal of Kurds on both sides of the Turkish–Iraqi border. Serious progress towards the establishment of an independent Kurdish state could create tension within, and even among, the states in which Kurdish minorities reside (Turkey, Iraq, Iran and Syria), and could threaten to provoke major regional instability. Ankara's fears have survived tension and conflict between the PKK and Iraq's Kurds, and have not been assuaged by Iraqi Kurdish cooperation in Turkey's war with the PKK. Since Saddam's overthrow, Ankara's frustration has been intensified by the limitations placed on Turkey's presence and influence in the region, the failure of the US to tackle the PKK in northern Iraq, the generally accommodating relationship between the US and Iraq's Kurds, growing Iraqi Kurdish control over a larger area of northern Iraq, and the receding likelihood of a comparably strong centralised Iraq emerging.

The Kurdish leadership's apparent appreciation that Kurdish autonomy might be better nurtured by an ethnically based Iraqi federation rather than complete independence dates back at least as far as the KRG's establishment in 1992. After all, Turks, Iranians and Arabs all oppose the emergence of a sovereign Kurdish state, and each would have the capacity to undermine its stability and security. Furthermore, Kurdistan is landlocked. The KRG has relied on transit across the Turkish border for humanitarian assistance, legitimate trade, and the smuggling of oil and other commodities. In recognition of these realities, a constitution drafted and adopted by Iraq's two Kurdish parties in 2002 envisaged Iraqi Kurdistan's incorporation into a loosely federal Iraq. On the other hand, it also insisted that the self-governing Kurdish area be expanded to include the oil-bearing provinces to the south of the current KRG zone that Kurds regard as traditionally Kurdish, that Kirkuk should be the Kurdish capital, that the Kurds retain control over their own armed forces (*peshmerga*), and that the proposed Kurdish state should have the constitutional right to secede from a future Iraqi federation.[30] These demands still stand. As Henry Kissinger has put it, 'Kurds define self-government as only microscopically distinguishable from independence'.[31]

Ankara and the approaching war

This was the background against which Washington sought to persuade Ankara to support its plans for military action to topple the Ba'athist regime in Baghdad. Turkey was requested to permit US forces to open a northern front launched from Turkish territory. Concerns over the possibility that an independent Kurdistan might emerge from the ruins of a post-Saddam Iraq formed the basis of Turkish opposition to American military action. Then Prime Minister Bulent Ecevit was especially outspoken in his opposition. As early as October 2001, in responding to a question on the possibility of US action against Iraq, Ecevit argued that, 'Turkey cannot accept this. This operation may lead to Turkey's dismemberment. It also will disrupt all the balances in the Middle East … We do not want any intervention against Iraq whatsoever. As I have stated, it will create many dangers'.[32] During a *Larry King Live* CNN interview on 16 October, he said that an attack on Iraq 'would destabilise the Middle East very much, and it could lead to the partitioning of Iraq, which in the meantime could create problems for Turkey, for Turkey's independence or territorial integrity'.[33] On 7 November, he bluntly declared to CBS that Turkey 'would not support' US action against Iraq.[34] At a 17 January 2002 press conference, following his meeting with President Bush, Ecevit said a military operation against Iraq 'could be catastrophic for Turkey, even if Turkey did not participate in it'.[35] The Turkish General Staff, to whom Ecevit was famously close, openly shared these concerns.

Such warnings continued right up to the eve of the US invasion of Iraq in March 2003. Indeed, Turkey's unease over US thinking outlived the change of government in Ankara heralded by the Justice and Development Party's (AKP) November 2002 electoral victory. The AKP represents a constituency more sympathetic to Turkey's Islamic character and its Muslim neighbours. Furthermore, few of its deputies had much experience of, or interest in, foreign-policy issues.[36] The election was fought and won largely on a platform of reform and rehabilitation of the crisis-riven Turkish economy. A related priority was the implementation of an ambitious program of political, legal and administrative reforms to ready the country for EU accession negotiations. With the Cyprus issue also demanding its attention, this novice government's political and diplomatic plate was more than full.

Official opposition reflected Turkish public opinion, which was overwhelmingly opposed to an attack on Iraq with or without Turkish participation. Indeed, former US ambassador to Turkey Mark Parris claimed that he had 'never met a Turk who likes this idea'.[37] On the other hand, as it became ever clearer that US military action against Iraq was likely, Ankara's discomfort was increasingly shadowed by a parallel policy aiming to maximise Turkish gains and minimise losses. This approach derived from the pragmatic recognition that all attempts to dissuade Washington were failing, and that Ankara's political, strategic and economic dependence on the US was too high to permit the luxury of opposition.

This duality in Turkish policy seemed to offer Washington possibilities for leverage. In particular, Ankara made clear its need for US assistance in guaranteeing continued IMF support to Turkey's troubled economy. However, Washington, far from acknowledging the need to accommodate Turkish concerns, apparently did not even contemplate the possibility of a Turkish refusal. It could be argued that Washington's determination to take action post-11 September, unilaterally if necessary, explains the US failure to appreciate its ally's differing interests and perspective and to make a more effective attempt to reach an understanding. Washington had no 'Plan B' in the event of Ankara's non-compliance, and Ecevit complained constantly that Washington simply wasn't listening.

This blinkered view was not unilateral. The Turkish government convinced themselves that, for geostrategic reasons, Washington would be unable to act militarily without Ankara's cooperation. Such thinking led Ankara to believe that it was in a strong bargaining position vis-à-vis Washington over the terms of cooperation, and that Turkey had an opportunity to ensure that their own strategic, political and economic interests would be attended to. US policy towards Iraq and the demands it made on Ankara, again in the words of Mark Parris, 'was testing the outer limits of strategic cooperation' with Turkey.[38] Ankara's regional sensitivities and interests, which Turks naturally regarded as paramount, were in contradiction to Washington's more global considerations and its sheer determination to act against Baghdad.

Pre-war bargaining

Ankara's concerns over regional destabilisation and the emergence of a Kurdish state from a dismembered Iraq led it to identify its so-called 'red lines', delineating potential developments that Ankara would deem unacceptable and which could even constitute a casus belli and justify Turkish military incursions into Iraq. These were contained in a leaked document bearing Ecevit's signature and code-named 'B.020'.[39] Chief among these 'red lines' was the establishment of a 'separate administration' by 'ethnic minorities in Iraq', which, the document declared, 'would be a cause for intervention on our part'. Also detailed in the document was Turkey's profound opposition to the incorporation of the oil-bearing regions of Kirkuk and Mosul in any future Kurdish self-governing region in Iraq. The document also declared the 'preservation of the rights of Turkmens as equal citizens of Iraq as among our basic political aims and objectives'. In addition to insisting upon Turkey's continued freedom to intervene militarily in northern Iraq to pursue PKK militants based there, Ankara identified lesser and more benign justifications for a Turkish military presence in northern Iraq, such as the supervision of Iraqi prisoners of war, the need to prepare for any repeat of the 1991 Kurdish refugee crisis, and the requirement to secure the Kirkuk–Yumurtalik oil pipeline that carried oil from northern Iraq to Turkey's Mediterranean coast.

Protection of Ankara's 'red lines' required that Turkish forces retain their capacity to act independently. Ankara refused to place any Turkish troops sent into northern Iraq under US command, and in its negotiations with the Americans endeavoured to limit the size of the planned US force.[40] Turkish forces on the Iraqi border were built up and put on an increased state of readiness.[41] Turkey also insisted that any Kurdish fighters armed by the US should be disarmed as soon as possible. Not surprisingly, the Iraqi Kurds threatened to resist any Turkish 'invasion' of KRG territory.[42]

As US–Turkish talks on access to bases and territory became increasingly earnest in late 2002, so they became increasingly tangled up in parallel negotiations over the amount of economic compensation Turkey should receive for its cooperation. Although the figures under consideration were not officially made public, it quickly became evident that the two sides were very far apart. In the wake of a National Security Council meeting on 31 January, the Turkish government finally agreed that on 18 February it would seek parliamentary approval for the entry of US troops into Turkey. The vote would be linked to approval for the despatch of Turkish troops to Iraq. However, the financial package, the number of US troops to be allowed in, and the terms of Turkish entry into Iraq, had not yet been settled to Ankara's complete satisfaction.[43] Against the backdrop of a diplomatic fallout in NATO over the despatch to Turkey of *Patriot* air defence systems, AWACS aircraft, and chemical and biological defence units, an increasingly impatient US was obliged to engage in frustrating and sometimes bizarre last-minute negotiations with Ankara over these outstanding issues. Even the terms governing the US personnel involved in upgrading bases was still a source of a great deal of technical, legal and financial haggling before they were actually able to begin work.[44]

As 18 February approached, Ankara was still haggling over the US offer of financial compensation, despite an increased offer from $4 billion to $6bn in aid and up to $20bn in grants and loans. Ankara was also resisting Washington's attempts to ensure that the terms of the deal should fall within the IMF rescue package for Turkey, and was introducing to the agenda items such as duties on Turkish textile exports to the US and the requirement that the aid package have a written guarantee attached in the hope that any future congressional opposition might be overcome.[45]

Given that opinion polls suggested that 90% of the Turkish population were opposed to a war with Iraq,[46] and that many AKP deputies shared this opposition, the granting of the requisite parliamentary permission for the entry of US troops onto Turkish soil was clearly not a foregone conclusion. The AKP leadership was aware of this, but was ultimately apprehensive about being held responsible for thwarting Washington's will, so did what it could to secure a positive vote. By March 2003, four or five US ships carrying tanks and other heavy equipment for the US Army's 4th Infantry Division were sitting off the Turkish coastline, and another 30 or so ships were on their way. Both the Turkish populace and government were manifestly unenthusiastic about the planned US invasion, and President Ahmet Sezer was voicing his concerns over the legality of Turkish involvement.[47] Against a backdrop of increasing frustration in Washington, on 26 February, the Turkish government introduced a measure to parliament that would permit the entry of 62,000 US troops, 255 jet aircraft and 65 helicopters, for a period of 6 months. On 1 March, after more delay, and in the immediate wake of a National Security Council (NSC) meeting at which the powerful Turkish military had remained emphatically mute, parliament rejected the measure. In fact, more deputies voted for than against the measure (all of them AKP), but abstentions ensured the bill failed its passage by just three votes.[48]

Denied the opportunity to commit around 30% of its assembled force at the outset of the war, unable to approach the Sunni heartland from the north, obliged to deploy its 4th infantry logistical supply chain by sea to the Gulf, and frustrated by Ankara's negotiating tactics and refusal to comply, the US government was incensed. Feeling ran particularly high in the Pentagon, hitherto Ankara's main institutional ally in Washington. The then Assistant Secretary for Defense, Paul Wolfowitz, whose responsibility it had been to coax Ankara into supporting Washington's war plans, suggested in an interview with CNN-Turkey in early May 2003 that Turkey apologise for its mistake in refusing the entry of US troops, and chided Turkey's military leadership for failing to exercise leadership by lobbying more actively for a positive parliamentary vote.[49] Wolfowitz's comments caused uproar in Turkey,[50] and provoked Prime Minister Recep Erdogan to declare that, 'Turkey, from the beginning, made no mistakes.'[51] Ironically, the Turkish military leadership itself queried whether a more assertive military role would have been compatible with Turkey's democratic processes.[52]

Undoubtedly, there were tactical errors on the Turkish side and a degree of mutual misperception. Yet Washington appeared to be in denial about the depth of Ankara's opposition right across the political spectrum and overwhelmingly shared by the public.[53] The US did not take sufficient note of the fact that the TGS was at best lukewarm about US plans and was preparing a dramatic intervention of its own in northern Iraq. Americans did not appreciate the seriousness of Turkey's concern about the Kurdish issue and the extent to which their own readiness to arm, train and operate with the Iraqi Kurdish *peshmerga* was seen as threatening by Ankara. The US failed to assess the nature of the new AKP government and did not take sufficient account of the domestic political difficulties it was experiencing in its endeavours to cooperate with the US.

Nor had Washington learned from history. In 1990, President Turgut Ozal stood against much of Turkey's policy elite in so wholeheartedly supporting the coalition effort against Iraq, even though Turkey was not being asked to host US ground troops and was not necessarily expected to contribute troops of its own. Indeed, such was the discomfort with Ozal's behaviour that it helped provoke the resignation of Turkey's Chief of the General Staff General Necip Torumtay, and possibly those of the foreign and defence ministers too.[54] Without Ozal it is possible, even probable, that Turkish support for the coalition effort in 1990–91 would not have been forthcoming. Turks have complained subsequently about the negative economic consequences for the Turkish economy stemming from Ozal's closure of the oil pipelines from northern Iraq and its participation in trade sanctions against Iraq, a major trading partner. Indeed, Ankara's demand for economic compensation during the talks leading up to the March 2003 attack on Iraq were transparently driven by Turkey's conviction that its sacrifices during the previous war against Iraq had been neither recognised nor compensated.

In the event, an undisclosed number of Turkish troops did cross the border in March 2003 to join those already in place. Iraqi Kurds, with whom US special forces were now embedded, threatened to resist them. US Defense Secretary Donald Rumsfeld announced that 'we have advised the Turkish government and the Turkish armed forces that it would be notably unhelpful if they went into the north in large numbers'.[55] As a result of the no-vote, Ankara's influence both in Washington and northern Iraq has been weakened, and Turkish foreign policy is still struggling to adapt to this new predicament.

CHAPTER TWO

The Kurds and post-Saddam political arrangements in Iraq

The interim constitution, or Transitional Administrative Law (TAL), that was unveiled in March 2004 was generally regarded as favourable to the Kurds.[1] The TAL provides the constitutional basis upon which Iraq is governed until a permanent constitution emerges from the transitional assembly elected in January 2005. It recognises the KRG as the official government for the interim period of the three ethnically Kurdish northern Iraqi provinces and thus, the ethnically federal nature of Iraq's transitional administration. Kurdish is designated as one of Iraq's two official languages along with Arabic. The Kurdish *peshmerga,* the largest of Iraq's private militias, are permitted by the TAL to function as the internal security and police force in the KRG zone. The TAL affords considerable scope for local law to prevail above federal law, and states that a referendum on a permanent constitution would fail if two-thirds of the voters in three or more governorates were to reject it, thereby giving the Kurds a veto over acceptance of a new constitution.

The TAL deferred the fate of the ethnically mixed and contested city of Kirkuk and its surrounding countryside until after 'a fair and transparent census has been conducted and the permanent constitution has been ratified'.[2] The Kurds, who are intent on the further 'Kurdification' of Kirkuk before any census is held, welcomed the postponement of a census initially earmarked for October 2004.[3] The TAL allows for some managed resettlement back to their place of origin both for Kurds displaced by Saddam's 'Arabisation' of the north and of Arabs (mostly Shi'ite) who moved there as a consequence of it, but gave no time-line for this process. Interestingly, given Kirkuk's contested future, the TAL expressly forbids Kirkuk (and Baghdad) the freedom to amalgamate with other governorates to form a region.

The Kurdish readiness to participate in a future Iraqi federation and defer decisions concerning the future of Kirkuk were insufficient to assuage the doubts of non-Kurdish Iraqis.[4] Ankara too expressed queasiness concerning some of the provisions of the TAL, and reiterated its concerns about Kurdish aspirations to Washington.[5] The strident Kurdish insistence on self-rule that provided a backdrop to the talks on the temporary constitution can hardly have generated confidence in Kurdish intentions. The Kurds had hoped that the permanence of Kurdish autonomy in a loosely federal Iraq could be guaranteed before the introduction of democracy. Their reasoning was clear: Kurds make up at most one-fifth of Iraq's population, and are greatly outnumbered by the Arab majority. Shi'ite Arabs alone constitute 60% or more of the population. This demography explained initial Sh'ite support for, and Kurdish opposition to, direct elections in the formation of the transitional assembly.[6]

The TAL does not guarantee that these interim arrangements will be carried over into a permanent constitution. Iraq's two Kurdish leaders, Massoud Barzani of the KDP and Jalal Talabani of the PUK, in an aggrieved 1 June 2004 letter to President Bush, expressed unhappiness with the draft US–UK resolution put to the UN Security Council in late May 2004, which aimed to restore formal sovereignty to Iraq when the Interim Iraqi Government (IIG) took over in June. They objected to this draft on the grounds that it failed to refer to the contents of the TAL or to guarantee that its main features would be made permanent. The letter threatened a Kurdish withdrawal from the central government if those provisions of the TAL that recognise Kurdish autonomy and self-government were not made permanent.[7] This threat was subsequently repeated on a number of occasions.[8] Shi'ite leader Ayatollah Ali Sistani, on the other hand, warned against including references to the TAL in the UN resolution, objecting to its references to federalism, the levels of autonomy it allowed the Kurds in the north, the scope it left for Kirkuk's incorporation into the Kurdish self-governing zone, the Kurdish veto over a permanent constitution and the inadequate role for Islam it implied for the new Iraq.[9] The Kurds were also unhappy that they were not allocated either the prime ministerial or presidency posts in the IIG, even though eight members of the 33-strong IIG that took over sovereignty from the Coalition Provisional Authority in June 2004 were ethnic Kurds.

Expanding Kurdish power

In the war to remove Saddam, Kurdish *peshmerga* cooperated closely with US forces in the north, engaging with Iraqi forces and those of the extreme Islamic group al-Ansar alongside US troops, liberating Mosul and Kirkuk, handing nominal control of these areas over to American forces, and ensuring that the areas under their control were secured.[10] The US invitation to Turkey to despatch a team of military observers into Kirkuk helped relax the tension in Ankara.[11] But the reference to Kirkuk as a 'Kurdish' city by Washington's interim governor in Iraq, General Jay Garner,[12] the election of a Kurd-dominated interim authority in Kirkuk,[13] and Turkmen allegations that the US favoured the Kurds,[14] made Washington's new, heightened regard for the Kurds all too clear to Ankara.

In an effort to strengthen their control and bargaining position, and to minimise the scope for intra-Kurdish dispute, the KRG's two governing parties have sought to integrate their otherwise quite distinct administrations.[15] In December 2004, they announced the creation of a single Kurdish electoral list to contest both the January Iraqi national election and the simultaneous vote for the 111-member Kurdish Assembly, as required by the TAL agreement (the first such election since 1992). Some smaller Kurdish parties, such as the Kurdistan Islamic Movement, and Assyrian and Turkmen representatives (but none from the Ankara-backed Iraqi Turkmen Front, or ITF) were incorporated into the joint list. According to PUK leader Talabani, Arab parties had not been included because none could be found that were sympathetic to Kurdish aspirations for autonomy.[16]

Since Saddam's overthrow, the KDP and PUK have enjoyed de facto control of Kurdish-populated areas beyond the KRG zone to which they lay claim, such as much of Tamim province, which contains the city of Kirkuk, and around Mosul.[17] Kirkuk, earmarked by the Kurds as their future capital, has been the primary focus of this bid for an enlarged Kurdish self-governing region. The city was liberated by PUK *peshmerga* in defiance of a prior agreement with the Americans before it was handed over to American forces. The US military engineered a power-sharing Kirkuk city council that included representatives from the Arab, Turkmen and Assyrian as well as the Kurdish communities. This did not prevent the Kurds gradually extending their control over the city and regional administration, however, including its police force and education system. The Kurdish parties have readily admitted they are behind this trend, and pay the salaries of the Kurdish functionaries that have moved into the city and surrounding area.[18]

Kirkuk also became increasingly inundated with returning Kurdish refugees who had been forced out by Saddam's successive 'Arabisation' programmes since the 1960s.[19] No exact figures are available, but it has been claimed that by November 2004 around 50,000 of Kirkuk's 200,000 'Arabisation' Arabs had left and been replaced by around 100,000 displaced Kurds.[20] Intimidation of beneficiaries of 'Arabisation' has accompanied this influx, although to a lesser degree than many expected.[21] There have been claims that some of the returning Kurds do not originate from Kirkuk at all, and at the end of March 2004, the Turkmen and Arab council members suspended their participation in protest, leaving a council of just 15 Kurds and seven Assyrian participants.[22]

Kirkuk, at the centre of an oil-rich region, has long been home to Turkmen and Arabs as well as Kurds. Indeed, it is regarded by many Iraqi Turkmen as well Ankara as the heart of the Turkmen community. Kirkuk's last census, held in 1957, determined that the population was 40% Turkmen and 35% Kurdish.[23] In addition to forced 'Arabisation', the impact of the oil industry has also done much to alter Kirkuk's traditional demographic make-up. Not surprisingly, Kurdish endeavours to reverse 'Arabisation' have caused demographic squabbles and ethnic tensions in the region. Turkmen, who as non-Arabs also suffered from 'Arabisation', have similarly sought to return to their former homes. These tensions have generated a more or less continuous low level of intercommunal violence among Kurds, Arabs and Turkmen since Saddam's overthrow, interspersed with more dramatic incidents. For example, following particularly fierce three-way battles in January 2004, US forces were obliged to impose a curfew.

In early 2004, the Shi'ite militants of Muqtada al-Sadr's movement began confronting the Kurds of Kirkuk.[24] Shi'ites constitute the majority of Iraq's Arab population, after all, and thus have a stake in a unitary Iraq that they could dominate. As the main beneficiaries of 'Arabisation', Shi'ite Arabs have suffered disproportionately at the hands of the Kurds in Kirkuk since April 2003. Many Iraqi Turkmen, perhaps 40% of the total,[25] are also Shi'ites. Towards the end of 2004, Sunni militants began targeting the Kurds of Mosul. A multi-ethnic city on the frontline between Kurdish and Arab Iraq, Mosul emerged as a major focus of Sunni opposition to the imminent elections and to the coalition presence in Iraq, particularly in the wake of the US November onslaught against Sunni insurgents in Falluja.[26] In the light of the unreliability of ethnically Arab Iraqi National Guard troops, the US deployed Kurdish *peshmerga* against the insurgents, nominally as Iraqi National Guard but bearing Kurdish flags and wearing Kurdish garb. In this guise, the *peshmerga* have also protected Kurdish communities and operated in villages undergoing 'de-Arabisation'.[27] These incidents of *peshmerga* activity serve to intensify inter-communal tensions, help tighten the Kurdish grip on the north, and fuel Turkish concerns about the Kurdish–US relationship.

Notwithstanding these developments, the programme of 'de-Arabisation' and 'Kurdification' promised, as a consequence of Kurdish insistence, by Article 58a of the TAL, has not moved as swiftly as the Kurds might have hoped, for a number of reasons.[28] The authorities have been slow to put into place an administrative system to manage the programme. Security problems have meant that officials, including Iraqi and foreign NGO staff, have been unable to work effectively. Many returning Kurds do not possess adequate documentation to prove their property rights, particularly in urban areas where properties were often rented rather than owned. Little provision has been made, or agreement arrived at, concerning the resettlement of Arabs affected by any 'de-Arabisation' of northern Iraq. Furthermore, coalition forces have frequently obstructed attempts by Kurds to intimidate Arab residents into leaving their homes.[29] As a consequence, many Kurdish returnees have uncertain status and are living in temporary accommodation such as disused army barracks, ruined houses and public buildings of various kinds. The process has not been assisted by the absence of an agreed time scale for 'de-Arabisation' – the TAL simply says it should be implemented 'within a reasonable period of time'. The Kurds will surely insist that this issue is addressed more expeditiously and energetically by Iraq's new government.

In November 2004, the Iraqi Kurdish leadership began toying with the idea that the local elections in Kirkuk, set to coincide with the national elections, should be postponed on the grounds that the provision of the TAL calling for a reversal of 'Arabisation' had yet to be implemented.[30] Their reward for this threatened intransigence was swift and substantial. Just weeks before the election, a deal was brokered with the IIG and coalition officials, allowing for around 100,000 displaced Kurdish refugees to vote in the Kirkuk area in the January elections. The deal also conceded that a census in Kirkuk should not be held until Article 58 of the TAL providing for a managed 'de-Arabisation' is first implemented, and more speedily.[31] Unsurprisingly, announcement of the deal precipitated an Arab boycott of the elections in Kirkuk.[32]

This deal intensified Ankara's anger as the election approached. This anger was deepened by the independent Iraqi Electoral Commission's refusal to ban participation in the Iraqi elections by two purportedly PKK-linked parties.[33] A few days before the election, deputy TGS chief General Ilker Basbug warned that the Kurdish influx into Kirkuk and their electoral participation 'could make the results of the election questionable … trigger an internal war in Iraq' and 'threaten the territorial and political integrity of

Iraq'. He went on that such developments could 'pose an important security problem for Turkey'.[34] Prime Minister Erdogan and Foreign Minister
Abdullah Gul both swiftly and unambiguously supported the general's
remarks. Erdogan warned that 'the effects of any misstep in Kirkuk could
endanger the future peace in Iraq' and that 'the US and other coalition
forces … will have to pay for the negative events that could happen in the
future'. Gul warned that Turkey should not be expected to remain passive
in the event of internal disarray in Iraq as a consequence of developments
in Kirkuk.[35] He wrote to UN Secretary-General Kofi Annan warning of
Turkey's displeasure at the potential impact of handing the vote to Kurdish
refugees in northern Iraq.[36] On the basis of this Kurdish influx into Kirkuk
and the Sunni Arab boycott of the elections Ankara has questioned the
validity of the January vote. Although Ankara has yet to fully act on the
'red lines' identified in the months preceding the US-led attack on Iraq,
rhetorically at least the Turks have yet to forsake them.

Ankara's frustration no doubt rose further in the face of the ethnically Kurdish (and KDP member) IIG Foreign Minister Hoshyar Zebari's
observation that 'no country has the right to speak out on Kirkuk. The
people of Iraq will decide on the fate of Kirkuk'.[37] A few days earlier, US
State Department spokesman Richard Boucher issued a statement which
affirmed Washington's position that

> efforts to remedy the unjust policies of the Saddam government in and around
> Kirkuk, which included the forced deportation of residents, confiscation of
> property and the manipulation of administrative boundaries, are internal
> issues for Iraqis to decide. The Transitional Administrative Law (TAL), which
> was drafted and agreed to by Iraqis, lays out specific steps to undo Saddam
> Hussein's terrible legacy. The United States supports the full implementation of
> the Transitional Administrative Law, including Article 58 related to Kirkuk.[38]

The Kurds have not retreated from their key demands: that the KRG zone
be extended and that Kirkuk becomes its capital. PUK leader Talabani has
described Kirkuk as 'the Jerusalem of Kurdistan'.[39] KDP leader Massoud
Barzani has been particularly obdurate. During a meeting with Colonel
Lloyd Miles, the US military commander in the Kirkuk region, Barzani is
reported to have said that 'we are ready to take great risks … but we will
not accept the Arabisation of Kirkuk'.[40] During an October 2004 visit to
Syria – a country which, like Turkey, regards the prospect of an independent Kurdish state in northern Iraq as an unacceptable 'red line'[41] – Barzani
told a press conference that Kirkuk would eventually be incorporated into

Iraqi Kurdistan.[42] Though being careful to point out that Iraqi Kurds sought a federation with, not complete independence from, Iraq, he also reminded his Syrian hosts that 'Kirkuk is an Iraqi Kurd city. The question of this city is an internal Iraqi affair, neighbouring countries should not interfere'.[43] A few days earlier he made similar comments in Ankara.[44] Barzani has also warned that the Kurds would not feel obliged to protect Iraq's unity if their demand for a federation is refused.[45] In an interview granted on the very eve of the election, KRG Prime Minister Nechirvan Barzani again reaffirmed that acquisition of Kirkuk remained a non-negotiable Kurdish objective.[46] There have been frequent and equally uncompromising restatements of this Kurdish position since the elections took place in January 2005.

Notwithstanding this 'Kurdification' of Iraq's north, there are indications that the Kurdish leadership may have gone out on a limb with their own constituency in not aiming for full Kurdish independence and in not insisting on the immediate enlargement of the Kurdish self-governing zone to incorporate Kirkuk. One study has concluded that 'the Kurdish leadership potentially faces the wrath of the combined power of the Kurdish street and Kurdish diaspora'.[47] Indeed, although the leadership seems to have accepted, for the time being, the inadvisability of openly campaigning for an independent Kurdistan, few observers doubt the broader popular desire for the establishment of a sovereign Kurdish state carved out of Iraq's north. Numerous demonstrations have taken place both within the KRG zone and in Kirkuk in support of full Kurdish independence and sovereignty. A petition demanding a referendum on Kurdish autonomy containing almost two million signatures was reportedly handed to UN officials in December 2004.[48] It was claimed that almost two million people participated in an informal plebiscite, organised by the Kurdistan Referendum Movement, that took place alongside the January election in Kurdish areas of Iraq, and that 98.3% voted for independence.[49] Observer Peter Galbraith opined that the Kurdistan Referendum Movement could contest Iraq's next election as a political party if the current Kurdish leadership offers too many concessions.[50] A Turkish observer recently estimated that 90% of Iraqi Kurds want independence but that 70% of the Kurdish leadership believes it to be an unrealistic objective.[51]

The fact that the leadership of the KDP and PUK have participated fully in US initiatives in Iraq since the demise of Saddam regime has failed to reassure Ankara that the Kurds are fully and permanently committed to Iraq's territorial integrity. Turks observe that repeated US declarations of fidelity to Iraq's integrity have not been backed up by a willingness to rein in a gradual Kurdish takeover of northern Iraq. Many in Ankara believe that Turkey's oft-expressed worst fears are now being realised.

Turkey's local allies: the Turkmen

One means by which Ankara has been able to muddy the waters for the present and any future Kurdish self-governing enclave in northern Iraq has been by championing the cause of its Turkic kinsmen in the region.[52] The rights of the Turkmen was one of Ankara's 'red lines' in their early opposition to US war plans in Iraq, and provided one of the rationalisations behind Ankara's pre-March 2003 preparations to intervene militarily. In addition to the obligations of ethnic kinship – which, it must be noted, have not always been paramount in Ankara's thinking towards Iraqi Turkmen[53] – the presence of the Turkmen usefully serves to dilute the case for or territorial integrity of any ethnically based Kurdish autonomous zone in northern Iraq, complicates a bid for exclusive Kurdish control over it and could serve to obstruct Kurdish control over the Kirkuk oilfields in particular, given the relatively high Turkmen presence there.

Ankara and the Iraqi Turkmen Front (ITF) have repeatedly claimed a population of up to three million Iraqi Turkmen, although many of them live in areas other than Iraq's north.[54] In the absence of a recent census, the real figure is disputed, but the US State Department and the Central Intelligence Agency websites put the figure just a little above half a million, and less than 5% of Iraq's total population. Both Ankara and the ITF have alleged discrimination against Turkmen in areas administered by Kurds. In March 2004, the remaining six ethnic Turkmen on the Kirkuk council resigned in protest at the Kurdish takeover of the city's administration, and at the scale and demographic implications of the Kurdish influx.[55] Although the ITF initially mirrored Ankara's preference for a federation, if federation there must be, based on Iraq's existing 18 administrative governorates rather than on ethnicity, it has also argued that if the Kurdish case for an ethnically based federal Iraq prevails, then the Turkmen too should enjoy a self-governing zone of their own, centred on Kirkuk[56] and the surrounding area, which, the ITF has claimed, has a Turkmen demographic preponderance.[57] However, the ITF scored just 16% of the January election vote in Tamim province. Turkmen have also campaigned to reverse the 'Arabisation' of former Turkmen villages and homes, but they are disadvantaged by comparison to Kurdish groups, who are better organised and more numerous. Furthermore, a recent study found that 'the Americans put a tight noose on Turkmen activities and Turkish assistance to them'.[58]

Ankara's sponsorship of the ITF, reportedly a creation of Turkey's security services in 1995,[59] has caused irritation to Turkey's relations with the Iraqi Kurds, the US and even many of Iraq's Turkmen. It has been claimed that Turkish security forces have been present in the Turkmen areas of northern Iraq since the early 1990s, and began training and arming Turkmen fighters in 2001.[60] The ITF's leaders have been a regular presence in the corridors of power in Ankara since its foundation in May 1995. Washington and Iraqi Kurds are equally mistrustful of the ITF's links with Ankara; Washington refused to allow ITF representation on the Iraqi Governing Council appointed by the CPA in 2003 and superseded by the IIG in June 2004.[61] The IGC and the IIG each had only one ethnic Turkmen member, in neither case affiliated to the ITF. Ankara has also objected to Washington that the TAL, in identifying only Arabic and Kurdish as the official languages of Iraq, pays insufficient attention to the rights of Turkmen as the third-largest ethnic group in the country.

The '4 July' 2003 incident, in which US troops detained a group of Turkish special forces officers and Turkmen in Suleymaniyah on suspicion of plotting to assassinate the Kurdish governor of Kirkuk, amply illustrated the dangers of Ankara's continued active support for the Turkmen in northern Iraq.[62] In autumn 2003, the TGS proposed that the 10,000 troops it envisaged contributing to peacekeeping in Iraq should remain within a 150-kilometre range of the Iraq–Turkish border for 'logistical reasons'; this would have entailed their presence on large chunks of KRG territory and many Turkmen-populated areas.[63] This prompted the Kurds to threaten armed resistance and the Americans to propose alternative locations for Turkish peacekeeping duties.

A US assault, alongside Kurdish *peshmerga*, in the largely Turkmen town of Tal Afar in September 2004 elicited vituperative Turkish criticism. The Americans claimed that the town had been overrun by insurgents crossing into Iraq from Syria. There were also hints that US forces had acted at the behest of regional officials in this otherwise predominantly Kurdish area. Whatever the truth, Ankara expressed concern at the fate of Tal Afar's Turkmen population, and Gul threatened that, if the US-led assault was not terminated 'Turkey's cooperation on issues regarding Iraq will come to a stop', which immediately prompted a US request for clarification. Eventually, the Americans and Turks agreed to cooperate in providing humanitarian aid to the inhabitants, and Ankara insisted that the town's security should remain in Turkmen hands, but this brief and bloody incident has never been fully clarified.[64] Tal Afar has been Ankara's preferred location for a second border gate on the Turkish–Iraqi border, a virtue being that it could be controlled by local Turkmen rather than the KDP, with the added bonus of providing them a source of income.[65]

In general, Iraqi Turkmen have exhibited little political unity either before or since Saddam's overthrow, for a combination of reasons: their

geographical dispersal around the country and high degree of urbanisa-
tion, their relatively high degree of integration into Iraqi society generally, and because around 60% of Iraqi Turkmen, like the Arab majority,
are Shia. The Turkmen have often affiliated to ethnic parties other than
the ITF, or have identified as Shia rather than ethnically, with a section of
the community even throwing in their lot with Muqtada al-Sadr. Turkmen
have even occasionally claimed that the main problems they face in northern Iraq are not posed by Kurds but are the consequences of 'Arabisation'
and Arab reluctance to recognise Turkmen rights.[66] PUK leader Talabani
has pushed the same line with Ankara, to reassure the Turkish government
that a Kirkuk incorporated into a Kurdish federal region would be 'a city
of brotherhood' in which the rights of all communities would be respected
and power would be shared.[67]

A Turkish commentator has insisted that 'Turkey has to realise that
the Turkmens have not been able to forge any kind of unity or set up
viable organisations to become a political force in Iraq. On the contrary a
weak Turkmen Front has not been constructive in bringing the Turkmen
together, and the Turkmen Shi'ites have preferred to join forces with the
other Shi'ites of Iraq'.[68] Yet Ankara has persisted in championing the
rights of Turkmen. It continues to issue strident warnings to the Kurds
and the US that Ankara is committed to their protection and to ensuring
that Kirkuk's future must be multiethnic and not exclusively Kurdish, and
therefore cannot be regarded as an exclusively internal matter.[69] Again,
Ankara's rhetorical commitment to its 'red lines' appears intact, although
it remains to be seen how far Ankara will go in championing the Turkmen
in the event of a major crisis over Iraq's integrity.

Turkey's allies in the opposition to Iraqi Kurdish ambitions

The election of an AKP government instinctively more comfortable with
Turkey's Middle Eastern neighbours and character has coincided with
Ankara's conduct of an uncharacteristically active regional diplomacy.[70] If
sustained, this could have major ramifications for Turkey's foreign-policy
alignments into the future, and for its relationship with Washington in particular. Although Ankara's engagement with the Middle East has waxed and
waned since the Republic's foundation, Kemalist Turkey's stance towards
the region has been characterised as 'diffident and tentative', 'ill at ease', and
'located on the periphery'.[71] Turks 'have always considered the Middle East
to be a kind of quicksand that they would prefer to avoid. Turkish policy
has thus been to observe events in the Middle East rather than be involved
in them'.[72] Tensions over Turkey's secularism, its NATO membership and

its relationship with Israel, Iranian fundamentalism, Arab radicalism and occasional pro-Soviet leanings, water disputes with Iraq and Syria, the state sponsorship of terrorism, Turkey's former imperial domination of the Arab world, and a pervasive and mutual dislike and mistrust rooted in the Ottoman collapse, have in the past all served to constrain Turkey's capacity and desire for closer regional engagement and friendships.

Prime Minister Erdogan has promised a more active Turkish engagement, and asserted in January 2005 that Turks 'don't have the luxury of remaining insensitive to the problems in our neighbourhood … because of our geographic location, our history, our civilization and our national interests'.[73] It might also be that Turkey, sitting on the fault-line between the cooperative, consensus-building, Kantian 'security community' of a Europe with which it aspires to integrate, and a Hobbesian Middle East of violence, mistrust, terrorism and zero-sum approaches to disagreements,[74] is endeavouring to contribute to a climate in which 'engagement and dialogue, rather than confrontation and containment'[75] become the leitmotivs of its own and broader regional diplomacy. Developments in northern Iraq, and indeed, in Iraq as a whole, have been instrumental in propelling Ankara towards this approach, but may also be the main threat to its success.

In fact, Ankara's relations with neighbouring Iraq have long had a more pragmatic and cooperative character than those Ankara has enjoyed with most other regional states. Although there have been tensions over Turkey's control of the headwaters of the Euphrates and Tigris rivers, trade between the two countries was healthy until the 1990–91 Gulf War and subsequent sanctions against the Baghdad regime. Both benefited from the 1977 opening of the oil pipeline from the Kirkuk oilfields to Turkey's Mediterranean coast: Iraq because it offered an alternative to the Syrian outlet (of particular value during the Iran–Iraq war, during which Damascus's sympathies were with Iran); and Turkey because of the revenues it levied. Ankara also appreciated Baghdad's contribution to the containment of Iran and its tense relationship with the rival Ba'athist regime in Damascus, with which Ankara's relationships were also frosty.[76]

Former Prime Minister Bulent Ecevit has long been well disposed towards Iraq: he vehemently opposed Ozal's policy of supporting the US during the 1990 war with Iraq and subsequently, and during his spell as prime minister in 1999–2002 he campaigned for a softening, if not a complete lifting, of the sanctions against Baghdad. Under his stewardship during the late 1990s, trade between the two countries increased as Turkey sought to circumvent the impact of sanctions and further incurred Washington's wrath by entering into negotiations with Baghdad for the opening of a second border crossing.[77] Ankara sought to maintain a dialogue in the run up to the war, and repeatedly pleaded with Baghdad to ease the tension by cooperating with UN inspectors.[78] For its part, Iraq encouraged Turkey to resist US demands. The AKP government which came to power in November 2002 persevered with this open-door policy towards Iraq; even as war was clearly imminent, the Turkish trade minister led a large delegation of businessmen to Baghdad in January 2003, partly to drum up trade, but also to deliver yet another message to Saddam Hussein imploring him to cooperate with the UN.[79]

As US action against Iraq loomed, the AKP government – apparently without first informing the foreign ministry or the military – announced it would explore the scope for a regional initiative aimed at resolving the issue of Iraqi arms programmes without recourse to war.[80] Although some interpreted this move as aimed at demonstrating to the AKP's anti-war domestic constituency that the government had done its best, it also reflected a genuine desire to explore alternatives to conflict. To this end, Foreign Minister Gul embarked on a tour of Middle East capitals in January 2003, and secured agreement for a summit to be held in Istanbul later that month, attended by Egypt, Syria, Jordan, Saudi Arabia and Iran – an opportunity for Ankara to explain its perspective on the Kurdish issue. In fact, each of these states shares Turkey's nervousness about Kurdish aspirations, Iraq's territorial integrity and the prospect of regional turmoil. Nevertheless, the outcome was an inconclusive discussion and a weak final communiqué.[81]

Subsequent gatherings have been held in Riyadh, Tehran, Damascus, Kuwait, and Cairo. This loose regional alliance was incorporated into a UN Advisory Group by the UN Secretary-General.[82] With the advent of the IIG, Iraq was brought into this round of meetings. In November 2004, an enlarged meeting was held in Sharm el-Sheikh, Egypt, that included senior diplomats and foreign ministers from G8 states, senior representatives from the UN, EU, the Arab League and the Organisation of Islamic Conference (OIC), and foreign ministers from other states. In addition, at the Iranian government's suggestion, a meeting of interior ministers was held in Tehran in November 2004, aimed at improving security cooperation over Iraq. However, Tehran downgraded its representation at a meeting in Jordan in January 2005, in protest at Jordanian allegations that Iran was interfering in the Iraqi election in support of Iraqi Shi'ite groups. Iran is a powerful, Shi'ite, non-Arab state bordering Iraq, and has a Kurdish minority. For all these reasons, the Arab states involved in this multilateral diplomacy distrust Tehran's intentions, suspecting it of seeking to ensure a pro-Tehran and Shi'ite outcome in Iraq. This hints at the possible regional

tensions to come. With Turkey, much of the Arab world laments the passing of Sunni dominance in Iraq, and is equally nervous over the prospect of
the country's break-up on the one hand and of the possible emergence of a
theologically Shi'ite and Iranian-sponsored regime on the other.

Ankara has been particularly keen to align its position on Iraq with those
of Iran and Syria. Turkey's cultivation of these two neighbours has intensified in the wake of Saddam's removal and as Iraqi Kurds tightened their
grip on northern Iraq. The evolution of this three-way relationship could be
vital in determining Iraq's future and its regional implications, as all three
countries border Iraq and have Kurdish minorities. Bilateral declarations
in support of Iraq's territorial integrity and against the Kurdish preference
for an ethnically based Iraqi federation, border cooperation, agreements
on the training of Iraqi security forces and government officials, and cooperation on dealing with Kurdish activities, are just some of the fruits of this
diplomacy.[83]

In March 2004, both Iran and Syria were reminded of the potential impact
of developments in northern Iraq on their own societies. In Syria, Kurds
constitute around 9% of the population, of which 200,000 or more are denied
citizenship altogether. The Kurdish language is banned, and place names
have been Arabised. On 11 March, a football match in the Kurdish town of
Qameshli sparked riots and demonstrations that spread rapidly to other
parts of Kurdish Syria and to the cities. In another incident, security forces
used violence to break up an attempt to commemorate the gassing of Kurds
at Halabja in Iraq. Within a week, clashes between Kurds on the one side
and Syrian security forces and Arab groups on the other resulted in at least
25 deaths, and hundreds of Kurds injured or detained. Reports of disorder,
detentions and deaths continue to seep out of Syria.[84] Large-scale demonstrations were held in several Iranian towns by Kurds celebrating the signing of
Iraq's interim federal constitution. Discrimination against Kurds, who make
up around 15% of the population, is more informal in Iran than elsewhere,
and is as much aimed at their Sunni faith as at their Kurdish ethnicity.[85]

Turkey's relations with Syria have long been troubled by a number of
differences, including Syria's resentment at the incorporation into Turkey
of Hatay province in 1939, the contrasting Cold War affiliations of the two
states, Ankara's relationship with Syria's arch-enemy Israel, and water
disputes. Although Syria too has always maintained a watchful eye on its
own Kurdish minority, its readiness to offer a sanctuary and training facili-
ties to the PKK as a lever against Ankara added substantially to the frosti-
ness in Turkish–Syrian relations.[86] Relations between Ankara and Damascus
improved gradually in the wake of President Bashar al-Assad's expulsion

of PKK leader Ocalan in 1998. Since March 2003, they have warmed markedly, embracing frequent official visits that have resulted in economic and cultural as well as political and diplomatic initiatives. President Bashar al-Assad's visit to Turkey in January 2004, during which he proclaimed that 'we have moved together from an atmosphere of distrust to trust',[87] was the first visit to Turkey by a Syrian head of state. Ankara has appreciated Syrian cooperation in tracking down some of the perpetrators of the November 2003 Istanbul bombings and their associates.

Despite an imperial, even civilisational, Ottoman–Persian rivalry, relations between Turkey and Pahlavi Iran were nevertheless generally pragmatic and cooperative. The 1979 Iranian revolution ruptured this reasonably comfortable co-existence. Turkey's Westernising proclivities were now explicitly juxtaposed against the anti-Western fundamentalism of Tehran's theologically inspired regime. Iran opposes a US presence in the region that has often been facilitated by Turkey, and has been a fierce opponent of Israel's right to exist. Ankara, in turn, has often suspected Iran of inspiring and supporting Islamic fundamentalist groups operating in Turkey. The collapse of the Soviet Union offered new battlegrounds in which this rivalry could be expressed. Tehran has long been suspicious of the loyalties of the country's Turkic Azeri minority, and sided with Armenia (and Russia) over the Nagorno-Karabakh dispute in opposition to Ankara's sympathies for Azerbaijan's cause. Turkish–Iranian rivalry has also manifested itself in a low-key competition for influence in Central Asia, and in pipeline route diplomacy.[88]

During 2003, largely as a consequence of Ankara's overtures, Turkish–Iranian relations improved considerably. Security issues relating to northern Iraq and the PKK provided much of the impetus and content for these meetings, although economic relations and the wider problems of Iraq were also featured. Contacts have intensified, and during Foreign Minister Gul's visit to Tehran in January 2004, the Iranian President Muhammad Khatami declared that 'Turkey's security is our own security' and that 'Turkey's enemies, terrorist groups or others, cannot harm Turkey by using Iranian territory'.[89] Prime Minister Erdogan's visit to Tehran in July 2004 coincided with Iran's designation of the PKK as a proscribed terrorist organisation. There have subsequently been joint Turkish–Iranian security force operations against PKK activists on Iranian territory.[90]

US displeasure with the visit, and with Turkey's new-found regional friendships in general, compelled Erdogan to deny that his trip to Iran should be seen as threatening to the US in any way.[91] Turkey's regional diplomacy was stoking American suspicions – dismissed by Ankara – that the 1 March vote indicated a deeper realignment of Turkish foreign policy.[92] Washington's focus on what it sees as the uncooperative behaviour of Turkey's neighbours, Iran and Syria, not least their presumed interference in Iraq, has if anything intensified with the advent of President Bush's second term.[93] The harsh warnings delivered to Iran and Syria by Bush in his February 2005 State of the Union address starkly illustrated the absence of shared Turkish–US interests in or understanding of the region's affairs. It is hard to see how Ankara's ever-warmer engagement with Syria and Iran can continue without a corresponding cooling in its relations with Washington.

Ankara's efforts to re-engage more constructively with its Middle Eastern neighbours have been accompanied by a more proactive approach to its relations with the wider Islamic world. This too has been partly prompted by Turkey's search for an outcome more to its liking in Iraq, but it also reflects the deeper instincts of the AKP. One illustration of this was Foreign Minister Gul's call at the OIC summit in Malaysia in October 2003 for a peacekeeping force for Iraq drawn from the Islamic world. This initiative might have been motivated in part as an attempt to deflect criticism of Turkey's offer to send 10,000 troops into Iraq, an offer subsequently withdrawn in the face of opposition from Iraq's Governing Council and particularly its Kurdish members. In fact, Turkey's proposal received a cool response at the summit, with the Jordanian delegation arguing that parochial agendas and interests should disqualify Iraq's neighbours from participating in any peacekeeping force in Iraq. Most delegations took the view that an Islamic peacekeeping force for Iraq could only be put together under UN auspices.[94] Despite this setback, Ankara did make a positive overall impression on the OIC delegates; its reward, a year later, was the election at the OIC summit in Istanbul of the first Turkish secretary general of the organisation, Professor Ekmel Eddin Ihsanoglu.

The apparent cooling of the AKP government's relationship with Israel has further added to the sense that Ankara's regional alignments are undergoing a transformation. Amid an increasingly critical Turkish stance on Israeli policies towards the Palestinians, in May 2003, the Turkish ambassador to Israel was recalled in protest at Israeli behaviour in Gaza. In May 2004, Erdogan described Israeli's hardline behaviour in Gaza as 'state terrorism'. In July he cited his daughter's wedding as a reason not to receive Israel's deputy prime minister. More pertinent to the Kurdish issue was the claim in the *New Yorker* magazine, by the American journalist Seymour Hersh, that Israeli military and intelligence officers had been training Kurdish *peshmerga* both as a precaution against the emergence of an Iranian-backed Shi'ite regime in Iraq, and as a means to weaken and monitor both Iran and Syria.[95] Israel had offered humanitarian and military support to the Kurds in the 1960s and 1970s in their fight against Saddam, and there has long been sympathy in Israel for the Kurdish cause. There are around 50,000 Israelis of Kurdish origin, and Jews were generally well integrated into Kurdish society. Furthermore, the Kurdish plight – of a stateless and friendless people surrounded by hostile Arab nationalist regimes and Iran – strikes a chord in Israel.

Given that Turkey is the most determined opponent of Kurdish aspirations to self-determination, explicit Israeli support for the Kurds would inevitably upset the Jewish state's alliance with Ankara. The Hersh article, which claimed to be based on Israeli, American, Turkish and German intelligence sources, was met with a predictable official and media furore in Turkey, and Gul rather unconvincingly accepted Israeli and Kurdish denials.[96] Whatever the truth of the matter, it is conceivable that Israel would welcome the establishment of a Kurdish state as a means to weaken its adversaries and as a potential regional ally. Although both Turkey and Israel profess to value their relationship – and the fact that the annual joint US–Israel–Turkish naval exercises took place as planned in January 2005 suggest that the military relationship remains intact – there can be little doubt that the Kurdish issue contains the potential to further damage a relationship that has clearly deteriorated since the AKP election victory in November 2002.

The Kurdish Workers Party

Turkey's evolving stance towards events in northern Iraq is harnessed to the unfolding of its domestic Kurdish story. In April 2002, the PKK changed its name to the Kurdistan Freedom and Democracy Congress (KADEK), then again in November 2003 to the Kurdistan People's Congress (KONGRA-GEL).[97] These name changes in part reflected a somewhat futile attempt to evade international proscription, but were also indicative of internal rifts, with reports of a shift towards a non-violent approach by some leading PKK figures.[98] By mid-2004, there were thought to be an estimated 5,000 PKK fighters in the mountains of northern Iraq, mostly inside PUK territory close to Iran, and up to 1,800 inside Turkey. However, on 1 June 2004, the PKK's unilateral ceasefire of February 2000, which was never absolute in its implementation, was called off. This seems to have been accompanied by an infiltration of as many as 1,200 PKK fighters into Turkey from northern Iraq.[99] There has subsequently been a marked increase in violent exchanges inside Turkey between Turkish security forces and PKK units: between 1 June and 30 August 2004, 109 PKK attacks resulted in the 35 Turkish security officers killed and 94 injured.[100] Ankara believes this upsurge of violence has been facilitated by the PKK's freedom of movement in northern Iraq.

Since April 2003, Ankara has had little alternative but to become more reliant on the willingness and ability of US and Iraqi Kurdish forces to flush out PKK cells operating in northern Iraq. For Turkey's security and political elite, this has proved a frustrating experience. In autumn 2003 Washington agreed to an 'action plan', details of which were kept under wraps, but which Ankara clearly interpreted as obliging American forces to confront the PKK presence in Iraq on Ankara's behalf. There has been little evidence of a will or capacity to invest in this mission, which enjoys the declaratory support of the Iraqi Kurdish leadership. As early as January 2004, Turkish General Ilker Basburg, who had helped negotiate the agreement, was already declaring that 'the US's fight against the PKK is not meeting our expectation'.[101] By September, Gul appeared to have given up on US goodwill on the issue, and told a Turkish newspaper that 'we cannot progress on this issue by relying on other countries', and that Turkey will itself 'do what our security necessitates'.[102] During the same month, he reportedly warned Barzani and Talabani that the PKK issue could produce 'a calamity for you in the future, be aware of this'.[103] By November Gul was asking rhetorically, 'How much longer can they postpone the operation?' and declaring that the US had 'lost the Turkish people already' as a consequence of their inaction.[104]

The US position, reportedly made clear during the 'action plan' discussions with Ankara, was that it had other security priorities in Iraq; that searching out PKK activists in their mountain hideouts would be difficult, time-consuming and manpower-expensive; that Ankara was exaggerating the threat posed by the remnants of the PKK; and that in any case a more political approach was needed.[105] There would be no immediate military action, a position Washington has subsequently reiterated.[106] In August 2004, then US National Security Advisor Condoleezza Rice remarked under questioning that 'we are doing what we can with non-military means to try and make less active and less capable those forces'.[107] Erdogan declared himself unconvinced by these remarks, and went on to contrast the US onslaught against Fallujah with its inactivity in the mountains of northern Iraq.[108] More recently, Bush reaffirmed the American position to Erdogan[109] and the February 2005 visit to Ankara by then designate US Secretary of State Condoleezza Rice also offered no indication that the US yet intended to be more proactive in its approach to the PKK.

In fact, in January 2005, following a six-week period during which Erdogan appeared too busy to meet with US Ambassador Eric Edelman, behaviour widely interpreted as a snub to Washington, the first tripartite Turkish–

US–Iraqi meeting to discuss the PKK presence in northern Iraq was held. It appears that the Turkish side, having secured Iraq's consent that extradition agreements signed between the two countries in 1989 and 1995 were still in place, demanded that 150 of the PKK's leaders in northern Iraq be extradited to Turkey. However, immediate military action against the PKK was again ruled out,[110] as it had been by Ambassador Edelman in an interview given to the Turkish daily *Zaman* a few days earlier.[111] Rather, it was reported that the US continued to favour non-military measures, such as interrupting the PKK's financial flow and curbing its communication capabilities.[112]

Neglect of this issue will cause mounting discontent in Ankara, particularly if the recent revival of PKK violence persists. Failure to shut down the PKK, it was argued in autumn 2003, 'threatens Turkish stability, the future of US–Turkish relations, and even the success of Operation Iraqi Freedom'.[113] Whether one accepts this assessment or not, Turkish–US relations remain troubled by the issue, as evinced by remarks made by Prime Minister Erdogan in a February 2005 *Newsweek* interview.[114] Disturbingly, detailed reports began to appear towards the end of 2004 that the Turkish armed forces were again preparing to intervene in force in northern Iraq, partly to address the 'red line' issues of, in the words of a retired senior Turkish foreign ministry official, 'the fait accompli that might be created by Barzani and Talabani and its negative effects on the Turkmen', but also to get to grips with the PKK there, now rumoured to have recruited Iranian and Syrian Kurd fighters to its cause. The reports claim that the TGS had drawn up plans to insert 20,000 troops – scaled down from the 40,000 initially proposed – into northern Iraq some time after the January 2005 Iraqi elections, initially focusing on eliminating the PKK from the border areas. The plans were reportedly discussed at a meeting on 14 October attended by Erdogan, the chief and deputy chief of the TGS, Gul, his undersecretary and other foreign affairs ministry officials, at which 'a consensus emerged … suggesting that a more energetic policy and any ensuing appropriate action would be unavoidable in relation to northern Iraq'.[115] It was reported that Washington's approval was also sought.[116]

Integration of Turkey's Kurds?

Although the TGS does not appear to have modified its hardline approach towards the PKK, Turkey has recently witnessed some novel developments relating to its domestic Kurdish issue. At least initially, much of the impetus for these shifts has emanated from outside Turkey. Thus, in its endeavour to persuade Ankara to adopt a more flexible and softer approach, Washington encouraged the Turks to experiment with an amnesty for PKK militants.

Introduced for six months in August 2003, the amnesty offered relatively lenient sentences of between nine and 12 years for those who had committed murder in support of the Kurdish separatist cause, and waived sentences for PKK functionaries who had not participated in violent attacks. However, no concessions were allowed for those identified as PKK leaders. The majority of those who took advantage of the offer were already in detention. Few left their mountain hideouts to take it up.[117]

More significant has been the raft of legislation relating to the Kurdish issue introduced since 2001 as part of Turkey's EU accession bid. In addressing the human rights and democratic limitations of Turkish politics to align political practice with the European mainstream, these reforms will directly or indirectly alter the state's approach to its Kurdish problems. For example, the death penalty has been abolished. Military dominance of the National Security Council (NSC), hitherto a major vehicle for the military's imposition of its uncompromising security approach to the Kurdish issue, has been nominally ended with the appointment of a civilian chairman. Measures to allow scrutiny of the defence budget have been introduced. Military representation on media and education boards has been terminated. The military-dominated state security courts, frequently used in cases against Kurdish activists, have been abolished. The Turkish government has declared zero tolerance of torture by the country's security and police forces. Of more direct relevance, various pieces of legislation permitting education and broadcasting in the Kurdish language has been passed, and the first Kurdish language classes and legal Kurdish language broadcasts have since occurred.[118] The state of emergency imposed in ten provinces of southeastern Turkey in 1987 in response to PKK violence there has been lifted throughout the entire region.

It is a paradox of Turkish politics that the secular, traditionally pro-Western Kemalist elite, most particularly the military, have come to appear relatively lukewarm towards the EU.[119] There has been considerable resistance from the state institutions and from the AKP's political opponents, and many of the new constitutional and legal changes include 'get-out' clauses that give wide scope for the notoriously conservative judiciary to restrict in practice many of the freedoms that the EU expects to see implemented. Bureaucratic obstacles – often extremely petty – have been put in the way of the development of Kurdish language courses, and the freedom to broadcast in Kurdish is severely restricted. It remains illegal to speak Kurdish in any Turkish government office or to make a political speech in Kurdish. The Turkish registry continues to refuse names with Kurdish spelling. The EU has learned to distinguish between reform and its implementation in the Turkish case, and the capacity of the regional and central bureaucracies, the courts, the law enforcement agencies and the like to obstruct and delay the full implementation of the new laws and regulations should not be underestimated.[120] The November 2003 European Commission Progress Report drew attention to these difficulties, and exhibited a degree of scepticism with respect to implementation.[121]

Notwithstanding such caveats, the reforms do put some constraints on the capacity of state institutions to maintain their repressive approach to expressions of Kurdish particularism. The existence of Kurds as Kurds, with a language of their own, is now incorporated into legislation – or at least implied by it, given the absence of the word 'Kurd' in the wording of the new laws. The EU accession talks, which are to start in October 2005, will involve Brussels in close scrutiny of Turkish behaviour for signs of regress as well as progress. The political cost to Turkey of overt, widespread or officially sanctioned repression of its native Kurds could in future be very high. Turkey's Kurds know this, and their political leaders are consequently numbered amongst the most determined supporters of Turkey's EU aspirations.[122]

The Kurdish issue is now more openly and hotly debated in Turkey than before. The release in June 2004 of former Democratic Party (DEP) Kurdish MP Leyla Zana and three of her colleagues, imprisoned a decade ago for their activism, and her call for a peaceful and democratic solution to Turkey's Kurdish problem in the context of a devolved but unitary Turkish state, has added to this debate.[123] The Democratic Society Movement established by Zana and her supporters in October 2004 could in time emerge as the political expression of a movement of which the PKK is the subordinate armed wing, aimed at the drawing up of a new Turkish constitution guaranteeing Kurdish rights and that identifies Turks and Kurds as two constituent nations of the Republic[124] – rather along the lines of Iraq's TAL. Some Turkish commentators have noted that extending democracy, human rights and a higher standard of living to Turkey's Kurds might be the best way of minimising the impact on Turkey of any Iraqi Kurdish self-government.[125]

Chapter Three

Iraqi scenarios

There is a range of alternative outcomes for Iraq as a whole and for northern Iraq specifically, and a concomitant range of possible policies the Kurdish leadership could pursue. Certainly, the January election brought little evidence of a softening either of the Iraqi Kurd's insistence on autonomy, or their commitment to incorporate Kirkuk. On election day, KDP President Massoud Barzani declared that 'the people of Kurdistan have a right to their own state', and that he hoped to see an independent Kurdistan in his own lifetime.[1] Within days of the election, the deputy leader of the PUK declared that 'the Kurdish districts must be returned to Kurdistan, among them Kirkuk, if not, we will no longer be Iraqis'.[2] In addition to the intrinsic desire for national self-determination, the distance travelled by the KRG will not be reversed easily. Neither the Kurdish leadership nor the Kurdish people seem disposed to sacrifice the autonomy they have enjoyed for more than a decade on the altar of an Arab-dominated Iraq.

It is likely that the Kurds will succeed in creating a demographic, if not a sovereign, Kurdistan in northern Iraq. The success of Kurdish parties and politicians in the recent national elections has already indicated the extent of 'Kurdification'. The forthcoming census will surely reveal an unambiguous Kurdish majority in Kirkuk. Whether sooner or later, in a managed way in accordance with the TAL's Article 58, or more chaotically and cruelly, both 'de-Arabisation' and 'Kurdification' will continue. Of course, ethnically and confessionally mixed areas such as Kirkuk and Mosul could well develop power-sharing arrangements between the various groups, as will presumably happen in Baghdad too. Although the Kurds probably possess suffi-cient strength to impose their will by intimidation or force, they have largely chosen not to. Talabani recently reiterated his frequent promise that, even if incorporated into the Kurdish self-governing zone and under Kurdish majority control, 'Kirkuk could become a multicultural city, thus strengthen-ing the brotherhood among Kurds, Arabs and Turkmen'.[3]

However, this is a promise of Kurdish good government and respect for minorities, not an abandonment of the prior Kurdish claim to Kirkuk. If Kurdish demands are not accepted by the rest of Iraq and neighbouring states, would the Kurds simply surrender either (or both) the autonomy they currently enjoy and their claim to the remainder of 'traditional' Iraqi Kurdistan? The political survival and economic well-being of a future Kurdish entity in northern Iraq, whether fully sovereign or federated within Iraq as a whole, with or without Kirkuk, is at the mercy of Ankara and other neighbouring states as well as Arab Iraq. The future for the Kurdish areas of Iraq depends on three factors and how they interact. Each set of factors are dynamic, unresolved and difficult to predict.

The first of these are developments within Iraqi Kurdistan itself. Will the Kurdish leadership remain true to its professed commitment to secure Kurdistan's future within the context of a federal Iraq? Can the KDP and PUK leaderships hold this position against what appears to be an over-whelming popular Iraqi Kurdish sentiment for full sovereignty and inde-pendence? Will the Kurdish majority accommodate the non-Kurdish minorities of northern Iraq – the Turkmen, Arabs and others? Will these minorities be prepared to settle for a minority status in a majority Kurdish society, or will interethnic conflict, possibly sponsored externally, desta-bilise the region? And will the KDP and PUK continue to work together, or will they again plunge into the kind of internecine warfare witnessed during the 1990s and indeed, throughout Kurdish history?

The second factor that will help determine northern Iraq's future status is the evolution of events in Iraq as a whole. A recent study[4] has identified three scenarios for the country's future, which serve as a useful template. The first is 'fragmentation', described as 'the default scenario, in the sense that it best describes the tendencies [currently] at work' in Iraq. It depicts a downward spiral into civil war, triggered by some combination of Kurdish separatism, inter-communal violence, majority Shia ambition, Sunni aliena-tion, shortfalls in Iraq's reconstruction, terrorist insurgency, and opposition to the coalition presence and any Iraqi government associated with it. This could lead to a situation in which legitimate and effective Iraqi institutions fail to take root and coalition forces are drawn into a quagmire of violence.

At the time of writing – just before, during, and just after the January 2005 elections – Arab Iraq remains distinctly unstable. It is too early to conclude that a functioning Iraqi political system will eventually emerge into which the Kurds could integrate, were they in principle prepared to. Should civil war or, possibly more likely, violent chaos constantly threaten, the Kurds would hardly agree to disband their militias or risk their autonomy. The *pershmerga* would be capable of protecting the KRG zone's order and integrity, and could probably seize, hold and ethnically cleanse the rest of what the Kurds regard as traditional Iraqi Kurdistan if the Kurdish leadership so chose, though not without considerable bloodshed. Against a backdrop of Iraq's 'fragmentation', a relatively ordered KRG, enlarged or otherwise, could emerge – or, rather, endure – by default or by design as a fully autonomous entity quite disconnected from a chaotic Arab Iraq.

The second scenario offered by the study for Iraq as a whole that could determine any northern Iraqi outcome is dubbed the 'holding together' scenario. Under this scenario, depicted as 'the best the United States can hope for', power would be shared between Iraq's various factions within some kind of federal framework that balances Kurdish self-government against a functioning central government in which the Kurds participate. Kirkuk might retain its special status as a multiethnic region – albeit one in which the Kurds predominate – or could be incorporated into a Kurdish federal region. Its oil resources could become the property of Iraq as a whole.[5] If not without its problems, an Iraq able to muddle through in this way would be reasonably democratised and internationally recognised as legitimate and worthy of support. It would represent Ankara's best hope too, at least in the light of Iraq's current realities, even though it appears that some in Ankara are not yet prepared to countenance the unambiguous breach of its 'red lines' that Kirkuk's incorporation into an enlarged KRG zone would entail. A satisfactory integration of Kurdish leaders into the pan-Iraqi government structure would be both a feature and a prerequisite of this outcome.

The third scenario for Iraq is dubbed 'regional remake'. This scenario 'is the most transformative and beyond US or multinational control'.[6] It would presumably evolve from an internal fragmentation of Iraq, and could involve the entire Middle East region as well as Iraq's immediate neighbours. An Iraqi collapse could engender wider Kurdish bids for independence in Turkey, Syria or Iran; a Sunni-based Arab nationalist and fundamentalist campaign against all its adversaries, both inside Iraq and beyond; and a Sh'ite assertiveness that could affect Iran, Saudi Arabia and other Shi'ite populations in the region. As the study puts it, 'the Shia could awake to the geographical accident that has placed the world's major oil supplies in areas where they form the majority: Iran, Bahrain, the Eastern Province of Saudi Arabia and southern Iraq'.[7] Ankara's warnings to the US, from 2002 onwards, to desist from intervening in Iraq were partly based on this prognostication of a wider regional unravelling as well as on the possible domestic implications for Turkey's own Kurdish problem. Ankara could be proved uncomfortably prescient in this foreboding.

This scenario leads to the third factor that might determine Iraq's future, the behaviour of neighbouring states. There is currently widespread external involvement in the affairs of Iraq by state and non-state actors, not least by Turkey, driven by a wide array of competing and overlapping motivations. There is no regional support for the emergence of an independent Kurdistan, and endeavours to derail the prospect exist alongside a competition for external influence over the Kurds. There exists too a widespread Arab preference for some degree of Sunni Arab grip on the reins of power in Baghdad. This has led to varying degrees and types of sponsorship of Iraq's Sunni Arabs, based in large measure on the fear that the alternative might be a Shi'ite-dominated, Iranian-sponsored theocracy. Iranian perspectives on each of these possibilities are at odds with those of the Arab world. Moderate opinion throughout the region generally appreciates that the stability of Iraq and the region would not be assisted by a precipitous coalition withdrawal. Most would prefer that a departing US leave behind a stable and functioning Iraq. The more pragmatic elements in regional governments probably desire or intend some variation of the 'holding together' scenario. However, external interference in Iraq can be benign or malign in intention and consequences, and is compatible with outcomes akin to each of the three scenarios outlined above. The dynamic of events will help determine which of them is generated. Uncoordinated and often competitive external interference in Iraq's affairs could produce outcomes no one wants.

Ankara's opposition to excessive Kurdish autonomy, and the measures it has taken or threatens to take in support of its policy, has clearly had a restraining effect on the Iraqi Kurdish leadership, directly or via pressure from American officials mindful of Ankara's concerns. If Iraq does 'hold together', Ankara's threatening stance might perhaps take some of the credit. However, a wary Kurdish leadership will need to convince the Kurdish population, Iraq's Arabs and Iraq's neighbours to accept, in the words of an International Crisis Group (ICG) report, 'what amounts to an historic compromise: acceptance of an autonomous region as the maximum objective of the Kurdish national movement they represent'.[8] It might also require the Kurds to accept the abandonment of 'the exclusive claim to Kirkuk in favour of a sharing arrangement under which the city and governorate would receive a special status'.[9] Yet a 'historic compromise' along these lines could well be unacceptable to Iraq's Kurdish leadership itself, to Iraqi Kurds generally, to Arab Iraq, or to one or more of Iraq's neighbours, notably Turkey. What if the Kurds of Iraq are unable to find a mutually acceptable modus vivendi with the rest of Iraq, or Turkey, or both? What if 'holding together' proves elusive or undesirable for the Kurds?

This returns us to the first set of factors already identified above: developments within Iraqi Kurdistan. Although the previously cited ICG report argues that, in private, the Kurdish leaders appreciate the need for self-limitation, their strident public rhetoric is in favour of maximum autonomy and control over Kirkuk and the creation of 'facts on the ground' in the Kurdish-populated areas beyond the boundaries of the KRG zone. KDP leader Massoud Barzani presents an altogether less compromising and more consistent figure than PUK leader Talabani, who is more inclined to play to the US or broader Iraqi gallery.[10] Yet, Talabani's PUK *peshmerga* have been no less active than their KDP counterparts in encouraging and facilitating the return of Kurdish refugees to Kirkuk and the surrounding countryside, and in intimidating non-Kurdish residents into leaving.[11] The ethnically Kurdish population of the traditionally Kurdish provinces beyond the KRG zone is growing, while that of the Turkmen, Assyrians and especially Arabs is fearful and shrinking. If and when the officially sanctioned resettlement programme envisioned by the TAL is seriously implemented, 'de-Arabisation' will speed up even further. Both Kurdish factions insist equally that Kirkuk is Kurdish. At present, the KDP and PUK are working together reasonably effectively, although they remain distinct and competitive, and their efforts are often uncoordinated. Arab Iraq is unlikely to possess the strength to resist Kurdish demands for some time to come. In this context, only a historically unprecedented act of Kurdish self-denial and restraint, or pressure from Turkey and Iraqi Kurdistan's other neighbours, will be able to prevent the emergence of an enlarged self-governing Kurdish entity in the north. Kurdish self-denial does not look imminent.

Options and problems for Ankara and Washington

Henry Kissinger has plausibly speculated that, 'if Kurdish autonomy goes beyond a certain point, there is a not negligible threat of a Turkish military intervention, perhaps backed by Iran'.[12] Retired Turkish diplomat Nuzhet Kandemir has written that 'should the Kurdish factions continue to abuse the undeserved power and authority they have been given in the current circumstances, one can predict not only the eventuality of civil war, but at the same time an intervention by Turkey into northern Iraq with a view to preserving the territorial integrity and the independence of the country. This intervention could well be tacitly supported by Syria and Iran by staying neutral'.[13] A future draw-down of US troops in Iraq, or an Arab Iraq either in chaos or itself seeking to rein in Kurdish ambitions, might be seen as contexts permissive to Turkish military intervention. Preferring to avoid such a provocative eventuality, Ankara would not welcome a precipitate American military withdrawal. Iraqi Kurds would resist any Turkish invasion fiercely, a prospect that might itself serve as a deterrent. This would deny Turkey the possibility of turning Iraqi Kurdistan into a kind of northern Cyprus, compliantly semi-annexed.

A prolonged Turkish military presence in northern Iraq could elicit both global diplomatic opposition and mischief-making by neighbouring states. Turkey's neighbours might share Ankara's concern about the emergence of an enlarged and excessively autonomous Kurdish state, but there is no guarantee that they would respond to such a situation with enduring equanimity. The US in particular would be compromised, and could hardly be expected to stay uninvolved. Were US troops still present in Iraq, both Washington and Ankara would wish desperately to avoid a clash, which would clearly be a risk in the event of a full-scale Turkish invasion. Partly as a consequence of this, Ankara's rhetoric has been far sharper than its bite. Turkey did not invade in March 2003, and Turkish troops present in Iraq or just across the Turkish border were kept out of harm's way – as was also the case in Tal Afar more recently. Turkish forces have also been relatively inactive with respect to the PKK in northern Iraq.

Presumably, Turkey's military planners have contemplated the risks of a military move against the Iraqi Kurds. In any case, shifts in the civilian–military power balance in Turkey's domestic politics might mean that any decision to intervene would fall to politicians rather than to the military. However, statements made by AKP government ministers have been as threatening as those uttered by military spokesmen. In the words of a recent report, 'the presence of Turkish forces and the manipulation of the Turkmen factor give threats of military intervention a sense of looming reality by creating their own dynamic'.[14] On the day of the Iraqi national election, Foreign Minister Gul alluded to the existence of dynamics that could lead his government to behave in ways not initially anticipated or desired. Turkey had behaved with restraint, he insisted, but 'this should not be taken to mean that Turkey speaks out, issues warnings, makes its position known but sits back and watches developments, even if its warnings are not heeded … sometimes you may not wish to embark on a road but developments force you to take certain actions.' He also made much of the fact that democratic governments cannot easily resist popular passions.[15] The same report quotes a Western diplomat as declaring that 'self-inflicted damage is something the Turks are capable of'.[16] Time and the dynamic of events will tell whether Ankara's threats are hollow or not.

With the December 2004 green light for EU accession talks, Turkey is on a path towards EU membership. A Turkish military move into northern Iraq would surely halt accession in its tracks, although the reaction to Turkish protection of a secular Kurdistan against a theologically militant Shi'ite Iraq would differ from that to an unambiguous Turkish move to snuff out Kurdish self-determination. It seems unlikely that the AKP government, or even the TGS, would want to risk Turkey's EU prospects so dramatically. The prospect of EU membership functions as a restraining influence on Ankara. It cannot be ruled out, however, that events on the ground in Iraq, Turkey or both may provoke reckless decision-making in Ankara. In any case, Ankara's EU accession talks look set to be rocky. Continuing difficulties over Cyprus, possible shortcomings in Turkey's human-rights behaviour and its adherence to the rule of law, the daunting scale of the task of aligning Turkey's economy and administrative and legal regimes with those of the EU, the continued opposition of EU Christian Democrats to Turkey's membership, and the possibility of referendums in key EU states obstructing Turkey's accession could remove inhibitions on a more forceful Turkish policy towards northern Iraq.

Domestic developments in Turkey – for example, the election of a more nationalistic Kemalist government, or a more pronounced political role by a security-conscious TGS driven back to the political centre stage by Kurdish and other developments – could also produce a return to the kind of Kemalist policies that were prevalent as recently as late 2002. Direct military takeovers in Ankara look increasingly improbable, although these should not be entirely ruled out, given Turkey's historical record of military intervention and coup. Furthermore, an AKP government whose overtures to the EU were unrequited, and which felt that Washington had treated its stake in Iraq with disdain, could reveal a more nationalistic and uncooperative face. In certain circumstances, Turkey could yet revert to 'illiberal democracy'[17] and to a more Hobbesian approach to its regional dilemmas.

The impact of relations with Washington on Ankara's behaviour in northern Iraq depends largely on how US policy evolves. Clearly, the US presence in Iraq, its warnings to Ankara not to intervene, the US military's close and cooperative relationship with the Kurds, and the fact that 'the

Americans put a tight noose on Turkmen activities and Turkish assistance to them',[18] has constrained Ankara so far. Since before the March 2003 invasion and up to the February 2005 visit by Secretary of State Rice to Ankara, Americans have repeatedly reassured Turks of their commitment to Iraq's territorial integrity and opposition to Kurdish independence. Turks are not reconciled to the situation and have little confidence in Washington, however. As this study has demonstrated, Turkish frustration with American inaction towards the PKK has persisted. Turks have not been reassured about Iraqi Kurdish aspirations to control Kirkuk, and Washington is judged to have been complacent about this prospect, if not complicit. Turkish resentment over perceived neglect of Turkmen rights since March 2003 is undimmed. There is a pervading sense that US–Kurdish relations are too close for Ankara's comfort. Additionally, Turks feel that US policies are responsible for the chaos in Iraq, and that events show every sign of slipping from Washington's grasp. Washington's officially upbeat line is not repeated everywhere, and there is a sense in Ankara and elsewhere – even Washington – that events could spiral beyond US control.[19]

Furthermore, there is at least some truth in the assessment of a recent study of Iraq's formation after the First World War that 'ever since the decision was made to create Iraq as a unitary state, it has been a complete disaster for the people of that country'.[20] The study argues that Iraq's tragic historical record means that we 'need to ask if a state as originally artificial as Iraq can continue to exist in its present form in the long run without either a monarch or a despotic military government to hold it together'.[21] The possibility of Iraq's fragmentation has encouraged some US analysts to ask difficult questions and offer alternative policy options. Among the most eminent is Leslie Gelb, former Foreign Relations Council chairman, who has argued that the Iraqi state, created as it was from three distinct Ottoman provinces by the British, possesses no natural unity. Only the oil-less Sunni minority, who have dominated Iraq since its inception, have an unambiguous stake in its survival. Gelb has proposed that the US encourage a three-state solution to Iraqi disorder, and takes events in post-Tito Yugoslavia as his guide.[22] Henry Kissinger shares some of Gelb's pessimism about Iraqi unity, and has argued that 'it may be that like Yugoslavia, Iraq, created for geostrategic reasons, cannot be held together by representative institutions, that it will tend towards autocracy or break up into its constituent parts'.[23] He too concludes that 'a break up into three states is preferable to refereeing an open-ended civil war'.[24] Peter Galbraith, guided by his experiences as US envoy to Croatia, is another who has openly contemplated the prospect of Iraq's ethnic break-up as a least bad option – or, in his case perhaps, a positively desirable one.[25]

For better or worse, Iraq's break-up is a real possibility, and it is not necessarily worse than all other conceivable outcomes. Nevertheless, a fragmentation of Iraq would pose profound policy problems for the US. As Kissinger
has asked, would Washington be prepared to support an autocracy in Iraq,
the historically tried and tested way of holding the country together? What
would the American reaction be to any violent suppression of Kurdish aspirations for self-determination by Baghdad, were a future Iraqi regime ever
to acquire this military capacity – particularly in the light of Kurdish support
and welcome for the US in Saddam's overthrow? Would the US support
Baghdad in such a venture, perhaps materially, in the interests of keeping
Iraq whole? Can the denial of Kurdish self-determination be squared with
the Bush administration's intensified commitment to the democratisation of
the Middle East region, or indeed, with US and general Western support
for self-determination elsewhere, such as former Yugoslavia, the former
Soviet Union and East Timor? It will not be so easy in the future for the
West to wash its hands of the Kurdish fate, or to represent Iraq's Kurds as
little more than terrorists, as has often been the case with the PKK. President
Bush chose to herald his second term with a call for global democratisation,
particularly in the Middle East. Will this aspiration be allowed to fall by the
wayside should the Kurds, Washington's best friends in Iraq, seek to test it?
A great deal depends on Kurdish restraint, which itself both hinges on and
is a precondition for Iraq's 'holding together'.

It is not implausible that the Shi'ite majority will preside over a pluralistic,
tolerant, political democracy governed in accordance with the rule of law.
As the 30 January election approached, even the leading religiously inclined
Shi'ite political groupings were promising to abide by the tenets of plural-
ism,[26] and the immediate aftermath of the election saw all groups calling for
inclusiveness, especially of the Sunni Arabs, whose electoral participation
was relatively sparse. US Vice-President Dick Cheney and Defense Secretary Donald Rumsfeld have both discounted the likelihood of Iraq's Shi'ites
imposing a theocracy on the country or of acting at Tehran's behest.[27]

Nevertheless, a Shi'ite-dominated Iraq based on Islamic *sharia* law
would bring problems for the relatively secular Kurds. The interim constitution, while declaring that any law contradicting the tenets of Islam will
be impermissible, identifies Islam as only one source among several for
legislation in the new Iraq. However, the religious Shi'ite leadership may
resist these limitations in the future. The future role of Islam in Iraq was
heavily debated in the preparation of the TAL, and Shi'ite delay in signing stemmed in large measure from their desire that Islam should be pre-
eminent in the new Iraq.[28] Furthermore, the Shi'ite desire to maintain a

unified Iraq and to defend co-religionists formed much of the motivation behind the violence committed by al-Sadr's followers in the Kurdish north of the country. Should the Shi'ites adopt a more theological and less inclusive approach to governance in Iraq, the US might well question whether the emergence of a theocratic, possibly unfriendly Iraqi regime was worth the blood, treasure and American political capital expended on it, and whether such a regime justified denying Kurdish aspirations for self-rule.

A Turkish–Kurdish understanding?

It has been reasoned that 'if the choice comes down to either a collapsed Iraqi state, one dominated by an Islamist government, or a dependent vassal Kurdish state, it is probable that the Turkish government would choose the last of these'.[29] This could yet be the outcome. Ankara's response to the emergence of a de facto or de jure Kurdish state carved out of northern Iraq would not inevitably be military. Political changes currently underway in Turkey as part of the EU accession reform programme, incorporating a greater democratisation of political life, particularly as it relates to the domestic Kurdish issue, and including a diminished domestic political role for the military, might encourage the idea of an accommodation with a future Iraqi 'Kurdistan'.[30] A softening of Turkey's internal Kurdish conflict, and a further democratisation and politicisation of Turkey's own Kurdish movement, would probably be a necessary precondition for a less neurotic approach to Iraq's Kurds. Ankara would need to be confident that it could politically insulate Turkey's Kurds from the self-government enjoyed by their Iraqi counterparts. Ankara is probably also banking 'on progress in accession talks with the EU to reduce its Kurdish population's appetite for accession'.[31] Another necessary precondition is a continuation of the lower political profile adopted by the military as the country readies itself for EU accession. Turkey's traditionally security-driven, militarised approach to the Kurds, both domestically and in Iraq, might be replaced by a more nuanced and sophisticated policy.

A cooperative relationship with Turkey is clearly in the interests of a land-locked Iraqi Kurdistan, not least 'because in the end, the United States will leave Iraq and the Kurds will have to live with the Turks who will always live next door'.[32] Furthermore, political and economic access to Turkey would be a prerequisite for an Iraqi Kurdish entity to survive and prosper. An Iraqi Kurdistan could derive enormous benefits from good relations with Turkey; conversely, a hostile Turkey could physically threaten, economically strangle, politically isolate and even occasionally intervene in northern Iraq.

In the circumstances, it is not unsurprising that consideration has already begun to be given to the prospect of the establishment of some kind of formal or informal Turkish protectorate over an autonomous Iraqi Kurdish entity.[33] How seriously should this idea be taken? Firstly, in many respects this kind of arrangement existed from 1992 until the overthrow of Saddam in 2003. Paradoxically, Ankara's facilitation of the US–UK imposition of a 'no-fly-zone' over northern Iraq made a major contribution to the emergence of the KRG. Furthermore, Turkish security forces intervened in the KRG zone almost at will, and maintained a permanent military presence there. Part of Ankara's frustration with the subsequent turn of events has been the cessation of this relatively advantageous state of affairs. The justification for Ankara's repeated border crossings was the war with the PKK, in which Ankara often sought and obtained the assistance of Iraq's Kurdish forces, especially the KDP. That the US has thwarted Ankara's freedom to operate against the PKK in northern Iraq, yet simultaneously declared itself unwilling or unable to step into the breach, has not helped Ankara acclimatise to northern Iraq's autonomy and has provided political ammunition to Ankara's hardline elements. Washington and Iraq's Kurds have a role to play in coaxing Ankara into acceptance of the situation as it has evolved.

Turkish–Kurdish cooperation has a long pedigree in north Iraq. Both the KDP and PUK maintain offices in Ankara, where Barzani and Talabani are regular visitors, and both have travelled on Turkish diplomatic passports since the days of President Ozal. It was long an open secret that Washington permitted Turkey to indulge in sanctions-busting across the Iraqi border, with oil entering into Turkey in exchange for, in the words of the US State Department, 'non-lethal goods and cash'.[34] The KDP's control over this trade, and over the Iraqi side of the Habur gate into Turkey, was a contributory factor leading to conflict with the less well-resourced PUK in 1994. In particular, the location of the KDP's fiefdom on the border with Turkey puts a premium on cooperation with Ankara, but also offers scope for conflict with it. Ankara used its former sway in northern Iraq to take sides in the fratricidal KDP–PUK conflict in 1994. In the past, Ankara has perceived Iraqi Kurdish division – not difficult to achieve – as being in its interests, and there are no guarantees that it will refrain from encouraging on KDP–PUK divisions and instead allow a more or less coherent and unified Kurdish entity to evolve.

Since April 2003, Turkish–Kurdish cooperation has existed alongside tension and menacing rhetoric. This was symbolised by Ankara's condolences to the Kurds in the wake of the suicide bombing at a gathering in Erbil in February 2004. Attributed to al-Qaeda, the bombing killed 100, including a number of leading Kurdish political figures, and many of the injured were treated in Turkish hospitals where they were visited by Foreign Minister Gul.[35] Both Ankara and the Kurdish political parties have encouraged the flourishing relationships between Turkish commercial interests and the KRG and the newly Kurdish-administered areas beyond it. Turkish companies built the new Suleymaniyah University campus and have been granted oil-prospecting rights by the PUK, although these latter are not recognised by Baghdad (Baghdad and the Kurds have yet to reach agreement on who has the right to manage the oil fields). There have even been reports that Ankara has struck a deal that will allow 'Air Kurdistan' to fly into Istanbul from Erbil.[36] During wide-ranging discussions in Ankara in September 2004, Talabani offered PUK protection to Turkish truck drivers, who have figured prominently among the one hundred or so Turkish nationals murdered in Iraq since the invasion.[37] These discussions, which included leading KDP figure and KRG Prime Minister Nechirvan Barzani, covered issues such as a second border crossing, the PKK presence in northern Iraq, and the status and future of Kirkuk. The talks appear to have been constructive, although differences between Ankara and the PUK (although less so with the KDP who have often resented the PKK's presence in their area) with respect to the PKK were again evident.

In the light of the Iran-backed Shi'ite resurgence in Iraq and the Arab world's support for Iraq's alienated Sunni population, Talabani has envisaged a counterbalancing Turkish–Kurdish axis.[38] Ankara seems to have entertained similar thoughts. A fierce policy debate broke out in the Turkish government, Foreign Affairs Ministry and military in the wake of the November 2003 decision not to send Turkish peacekeepers into northern Iraq. One option considered was to accept the reality of northern Iraq's autonomy, but to ensure its economic and political dependence on Turkey.[39] In summer 2004, Massoud Barzani insisted that Ankara's special envoy to Iraq, Osman Koruturk, had indicated to him that Ankara no longer objected to an autonomous Kurdistan inside a loosely federal Iraq.[40] In de facto terms, Ankara clearly does now recognise the KRG's reality. One Turkish observer has even claimed to detect the beginnings of a debate in Turkey over whether its interests might best be served by being 'the midwife of Kurdish independence in northern Iraq'.[41]

In short, poor and oppositional Turkish–Kurdish relations are not a given. Given that Turkey and the KRG are secular, pro-Western, democratised and geographically adjacent, there would indeed be some underlying logic to a closer relationship. The Kurds would receive protection against a nationalistic Arab Iraq or any theological regime or chaos that might manifest itself; in turn, Ankara would acquire influence over developments in northern Iraq, keeping at bay any deeper Iraqi chaos, and perhaps preferential access to northern Iraq's oil industry. An Iraqi Kurdistan that did not encompass Kirkuk might be more palatable to Ankara. There is no doubt that Washington would welcome a cessation of enmity and mistrust between its two regional allies, Ankara and the KRG. Having said all this, the other, minimalist policy option considered in Ankara in late 2003 was merely to keep pressure on the Kurds until such time as Arab Iraq is again in a position to take control or the Kurds once again resort to civil war. This too appears to have informed elements of subsequent Turkish policy.[42]

Washington's ally?

The tetchiness in Turkish–US relations has yet to smooth out, notwithstanding declarations from both sides to the contrary.[43] An illustration of this was afforded by US Defense Secretary Donald Rumsfeld's February 2005 remarks that Turkey's March 2003 refusal to permit the opening of a northern front was 'unfortunate' and 'probably' contributed to the strength of the insurgency today because the Sunni Arabs in Saddam Hussein's stronghold north of Baghdad 'didn't really ever experience the full power of the US military'.[44] One observer suggested that Turkish-US relations are suffering from 'deferred maintenance'.[45] At a broader level, the Turkish media and public opinion is rife with virulent anti-Americanism. Recent research suggests that the Turkish public is generally hostile towards and mistrustful of the US and its policies,[46] and continues to oppose the US-led war in Iraq.

During the Cold War and up to the overthrow of the Ba'athist regime in Baghdad, Turkish–US relations were heavily coloured by purely strategic and 'hard security' considerations. Now, Turkey's strategic utility to the US is far less certain. Much depends on the outcome of events in Iraq and elsewhere in the Middle East, an unstable yet vital region. *Operation Northern Watch* closed down with the March 2003 invasion of Iraq. The base at Incirlik remains home to around 1,400 US servicemen engaged largely in support and maintenance duties, and is currently used for logistical support for and troop rotation of US forces in Iraq. Its future, under the wider restructuring of US forces known as the Global Defense Posture Review, is unclear. Consultations with Ankara have not yet produced any decisions.

From the Pentagon's point of view, Turkey's location clearly remains an asset. During his recent visit to Ankara, Deputy Defense Secretary Douglas J. Feith specifically denied Turkish media rumours that the US was again seeking permission to station fighter aircraft at Incirlik.[47] Turkish–US cooperation with respect to possible action over Iran's supposed nuclear weapons programme might have been part of Feith's agenda, however,[48] and Turkey is likely to be considered as a staging post whenever US military action in the region is contemplated. In the wake of the 1 March vote, which demonstrated that Turkey could as easily impede as facilitate US freedom of action in the region, the Pentagon is bound to have doubts. Gul's threat during the Tal Afar operation to withdraw Turkish cooperation and support will also have been noted.

Developments in this eventful and troubled region could yet push Ankara and Washington closer together – or further apart. US requests for Turkish support, and Turkish readiness to offer it, is likely to be on a more case-by-case basis. In any case, American forces now have regional alternatives, including Iraq, Afghanistan, the Caucasus, Central Asia and southeastern Europe. Question marks are also now hanging over the future of Turkish–Israeli relations, which have, in the past, largely been conducted by or at the behest of the TGS. The AKP government is less well disposed towards Israel, and much hinges on the future power relations between Turkish civilian and uniformed security policy decision-makers. It seems less likely that Washington can comfortably expect to exercise its influence through an-all powerful TGS, as has often been the case in the past. The TGS might be less inclined to support US policy and less influential than hitherto, and Ankara's influence in Washington will probably decline accordingly.

Turkey: bridge to the Middle East?

Given the more comfortable embrace of Islam in Turkish politics and society in the wake of the AKP's November 2002 election victory, and Ankara's more positive regional diplomacy in recent years, Turkey might at last be in a position to function as a model of an Islamic but simultaneously democratic and West-leaning state to the Middle East region and the Islamic world more generally. Following Saddam's overthrow, and the consequent removal of the need to contain Iraq, it was likely that US–Turkish relations would evolve regardless of Turkish–US differences and become, in Wolfowitz's words, less focused on military cooperation, and instead derived from 'the common values, the common beliefs in secular democracy'.[49] Washington has long held Turkey up as a model for other Muslim states to emulate, and this inclination will strengthen in the context of the Bush administration's aspiration to democratise the region as a means of stabilising it.[50] Up to now, however, the attractiveness of Turkey's domestic arrangements to other Middle Eastern states and societies has been greatly exaggerated, especially in the US,[51] and Ankara has been disinclined to offer itself as a model. In contrast, an AKP-led and diplomatically energetic Turkey widely perceived in the region as having put some distance between itself and Washington, could more plausibly present itself as offering an alternative way forward for this troubled region.

Foreign Minister Gul, while insistent that any reforms must emanate from within the region and not be imposed from outside, has expressed sympathy for the broad contents of the Bush administration's so-called 'Greater Middle East Initiative' and has repeatedly drawn attention to the need for regional transformation. He has argued that 'the Turkish experience might serve as a source of inspiration for countries of the region' and that, furthermore, 'Turkey feels a responsibility to work toward the goal of a bright future for the Middle East'. He has also claimed that, as a consequence of its unique cross-cultural heritage and its broad experience of multilateral and regional diplomacy, Turkey is well-placed to mobilise 'the dynamics of multilateral regional cooperation in the Middle East'.[52]

Gul first outlined what he has dubbed 'the Turkish vision' for the Middle East region at the May 2003 conference of Islamic foreign ministers in Tehran, where he argued that the Muslim world needed 'to determine the issues and shortcomings that continue to hamper our progress'. In this endeavour, 'rational thinking should be our guide'. He called on the Muslim world to strive for good governance, transparency, accountability, gender equality, and the upholding of rights and freedoms, so as to engender a 'sense of ownership on the part of the people of the systems they live in', and highlighted the need to reduce the corruption, economic irrationality, and instability in the Islamic world, so that progress could be made.[53] At the subsequent Islamic foreign ministerial meeting, in Istanbul in June 2004, he repeated these arguments and warned that unless in the Islamic world 'we take the initiative to put our own house in order, outer pressure would be felt'.[54]

In the post-11 September, post-Saddam world, a Turkish–US partnership could reap practical benefits. For example, Ankara's engagement could be instrumental in weaning Syria away from its somewhat defensive, often meddlesome and economically autarchic stance towards much of the outside world, and in reducing tension between Damascus and Tel Aviv. Recently, Ankara has intensified its endeavours to offer itself as a conduit for Palestinian–Israeli dialogue. In January 2005, Gul visited Israel and the Palestinian Authority (PA) area;[55] a few weeks later, the newly elected head of the PA, Mahmoud Abbas, visited Ankara and suggested that Turkey might assist the US–EU–Russia–UN Quartet tasked with encouraging the Arab–Israeli peace process. Erdogan recently told a gathering of AKP deputies that 'our geographic location, our history, our civilization and our national interests' do not leave Turkey 'the luxury of remaining insensitive to the problems in our neighbourhood'.[56] At least at the declaratory level, Washington appears to have no problem with Ankara's attempt to adopt a higher profile in the Middle East peace process.[57]

On the other hand, a more proactive Turkish engagement in the region is unlikely to lead to an entirely trouble-free relationship with Washington. Turkey might seek engagement with its neighbours, notably Syria and Iran, where the US prefers confrontation. Ankara is also likely to oppose further US military adventures in the region. It might distance itself from Israel, as recent cooling suggests, and align with the rest of the region's (and Europe's) perspectives on the Palestinian issue. Above all, should the Bush administration's support for democratisation in the Middle East find expression in sympathy for or acquiescence to Kurdish self-determination, the limits of any shared Turkish–US perspectives in the region may well be reached.

Turkey: between Europe and the US

At the NATO summit in Istanbul in June 2004, US President Bush remarked that Turkey's EU membership would 'be a crucial advance in relations between the Muslim world and the west, because you are part of both'. It would 'prove that Europe is not the exclusive club of a single religion, and it would expose the "clash of civilisations" as a passing myth of history'.[58] Such thinking has long lain behind strong US support for Turkey's EU accession. The US would also welcome and benefit from the contribution made by EU accession to Turkey's economic and political stabilisation. However, there is also a sense that accession might further aggravate Turkish–US estrangement, particularly if transatlantic relations remain strained. Ankara's diplomatic alignments might increasingly move in line with those of Europe.

To quote Gul again, Turkey's EU membership would 'demonstrate that the EU stands for common values and institutions rather than a common religion'. Turkish membership would spread 'the message of reform, modernity, moderation, and integration … to the wider international community'.[59] Thus, the December 2004 decision to commence EU accession talks with Ankara is seen by Turkey, the US and by some, if not all, EU members, as having import far beyond the narrow confines of EU–Turkish relations and as hinging on more than the political, economic and bureaucratic 'rules' of the EU club.[60] The AKP government's approach to the EU has been more accommodating and less confrontational than previous Turkish governments. It is an irony of recent developments that the moderate Islamists currently in power may have internalised Europe's norms more fully than their Kemalist predecessors and may be better placed to promote Europe's norms in society as a whole. The secular, traditionally 'pro-Western' Kemalist elite, and most particularly the military, have come to appear relatively lukewarm towards the EU.

Much could revolve around the future of the AKP government. At present, the AKP is riding high, and the opposition appears ever more unappealing, divided and ineffective. It is not hyperbolic to suggest that Turkey's prospects of genuine economic, social and political advancement have rarely been so good. One can reasonably surmise that the Kemalist establishment feels constrained in its scope for intervention in the political process by the AKP's domestic popularity and success, as well as by the possible foreign-policy implications of any such action. However, bumpy accession negotiations, developments in Iraq that prompt active Turkish involvement, or a downturn in the domestic fortunes of the AKP government could all undermine Turkey's reform progress and its prospects of eventual EU accession.

Turkey's eventual EU membership is not yet certain. There has been considerable resistance from the state institutions and the AKP's political opponents. The EU has learned to distinguish between nominal reform and its implementation in the Turkish case, and the capacity of the regional and central bureaucracies, the courts, the law enforcement agencies and the like to obstruct and delay should not be underestimated.[61] The October 2004 European Commission Progress Report drew attention to these difficulties, and demonstrated a lingering wariness with respect to implementation.[62] Politically, economically and in terms of governance, Turkey still has a long road to travel. Doubts about the desirability of Turkish accession rumble on in the more Christian Democratic areas of Europe's political landscape, and proposed referendums on Turkish accession in selected EU member states could derail the process. The continued differences over Cyprus also contain the potential to obstruct or complicate Turkey's accession.

The transatlantic rift that accompanied the US-led overthrow of Saddam's regime has yet to heal, and has implications for Turkey's future role and place in Western security arrangements. The December 2004 EU decision to begin accession negotiations with Turkey ordinarily could be expected to encourage a trend towards Turkey's 'Europeanisation' in Ankara's approach to foreign- and security-policy issues as well as domestic arrangements. However, in the absence of consensus on major issues within Europe, it is hard to see what practical form such a shift might take. Continuing tensions within Europe over the transatlantic relationship, and the limited commitment in much of the EU to playing and paying for an active world role, could force Turkey into an intensified internal debate concerning its foreign-policy orientation. As the UK's experience suggests, transatlantic fissures can complicate matters for Europe's more Atlanticist states. The outcome of any such debate might itself depend on Turkey's domestic political evolution.

Past form might suggest that Turkey would continue at the Atlanticist end of the European spectrum, but this might be difficult to sustain in the event of US hegemonic behaviour, particularly on issues of direct and local concern to Ankara.[63] Nor should a Turkey moving inexorably towards EU membership anticipate greater sympathy from its European partners than from Washington. This has rarely been the case in the past, and need not be the case in the future. Turkey's instinctive mistrust of Europe was reinforced by the crisis caused by the refusal of France, Germany and Belgium, on the eve of the US-led attack on Iraq, to sanction NATO support for Turkey in the form of anti-air *Patriot* missiles, AWACS surveillance aircraft, and chemical and biological defensive units. It is far from self-evident that a pacific and relatively secure Europe would embrace Turkish sensitivities and support conceivable Turkish reactions to conflict, terrorism and WMD proliferation in the Middle East. At best, only one of Ankara's feet will be planted within the European security community. The other will remain firmly in Turkey's crisis-prone Balkan, Caucasian, eastern Mediterranean and Middle Eastern neighbourhood. For Turkey, the Kurdish issue is here to stay, in one form or another.

Notes

Introduction

1. For the referendum figures, see Kamil Mirawdeli, 'Voting for independence; people of Kurdistan make their choice', *Kurdistan Observer*, 8 February 2005.
2. Press release regarding the results of the Iraqi elections, 13 February 2005, http://www.mfa.gov.tr/MFA/PressInformation/PressReleasesAndStatements/pressReleases2005/February/NO23_13February2005.htm
3. Statement of spokesman of the Turkish Ministry of Foreign Affairs Namik Tan in response to a question regarding Kirkuk and the participation of the Iraqi Turkmen in the 30 January election in Iraq, 28 January 2005, http://www.mfa.gov.tr/MFA/PressInformation/PressReleasesAndStatements/pressReleases2005/January/NO3_28January2005.htm. The ethnically and linguistically but largely Shi'ite Turkmen were historically concentrated in the Kirkuk area, but are now widely dispersed around Iraq. Variously claimed to constitute between 500,000 and three million in number, they have been championed by Ankara since the emergence of Kurdish autonomy in northern Iraq as the Iraq's third largest ethnic group and whose presence undermines Kurdish claims to exclusive control of the north.
4. *Ibid.*

Chapter One

1. All figures for Kurdish populations are approximate for a variety of reasons – the absence of recent or reliable census figures, ethnically insensitive data-gathering, dispersal, intermarriage, assimilation and registration of Kurds as other nationalities.
2. The term 'Kurdistan' will be used here to apply to areas where Kurds have traditionally formed the majority of the population. It does not necessarily imply sympathy with Kurdish national self-determination.
3. David Mc Dowall, *A Modern History of the Kurds* (London and New York: I.B.Tauris, 1997), p. 4. This passage is largely based on McDowell pp. 1–18.
4. Cengiz Candar, 'Turkish foreign policy and the war on Iraq', in *The Future of Turkish Foreign Policy*, Lenore G. Martin and Dimitris Keridis (eds) (Cambridge, MA: MIT Press, 2004), p. 53.
5. Abdullah Gul, 'Turkey's role in a changing Middle East environment', *Mediterranean Quarterly*, vol. 15, no.1, winter 2004, p. 5.

6 Gareth Jenkins, *Context and Circumstance: the Turkish Military and Politics*, Adelphi Paper No. 337, (Oxford: Oxford University Press for the International Institute for Strategic Studies, 2001), p. 17.

7 For an examination of this see Umit Cizre, 'Demythologising the national security concept: the case of Turkey', *Middle East Journal*, vol. 57, no. 2, spring 2003, pp. 213–229.

8 For a recent study of the creation of Iraq, see Christopher Catherwood, *Winston's Folly: Imperialism and the Creation of Modern Iraq* (London: Constable, 2004).

9 Kemal Kirisci and Gareth M. Winrow, *The Kurdish Question and Turkey: An Example of a Trans-State Ethnic Conflict* (London: Frank Cass, 1997), p. 85.

10 Gareth Jenkins, *Context and Circumstance: the Turkish Military and Politics,* p. 16.

11 Quoted in Robert Olson, 'The Kurdish Question and Turkey's Foreign Policy Toward Syria, Iran, Russian and Iraq since the Gulf War', p.102, in Robert Olson (ed.), *The Kurdish Nationalist Movement in the 1990s: Its Impact on Turkey and the Middle East* (Lexington, KY: University Press of Kentucky, 1996).

12 Gareth Jenkins, *Context and Circumstance: the Turkish Military and Politics,* p.16.

13 Robert Rabil, 'The Iraqi opposition's evolution: from conflict to unity?', *Middle East Review of International Affairs* (MERIA), vol. 6, no. 4, December 2002.

14 William Hale, 'Turkey, the Middle East, and the Gulf crisis', *International Affairs,* vol. 68, no. 4, October 1992, p. 691.

15 Michael M. Gunter, *The Kurdish Predicament in Iraq: A Political Analysis* (London: MacMillan, 1999), p. 118.

16 If Turkey had kept Mosul, there would be no N.Iraq issue, says Demirel', *Turkish Daily News,* 19 December 2003.

17 Nicole Pope, 'Cross border concerns', *Middle East International*, no. 683, 13 September 2002, p. 11; Jan Gorvett, 'A hugely unpopular war', *The Middle East,* no. 328, November 2002, p. 11.

18 Nicole Pope, 'Eyes on Turkey', *Middle East International,* no. 691, 10 January 2003, pp. 14–15.

19 Gunduz Aktan, 'If Iraq operation takes place', *Turkish Daily News,* 20 November 2002.

20 See David McDowall, *A Modern History of the Kurds,* pp. 184–213, for an account of Turkey's wars against its Kurdish population during this period.

21 See Murat Somer, 'Turkey's Kurdish conflict: changing context, and domestic and regional implications', *Middle East Journal,* vol. 58, no. 2, spring 2004, p. 249.

22 For an account of the emergence and nature of the PKK and its leader Ocalan, see Henri J. Barkey and Graham E. Fuller, *Turkey's Kurdish Question* (Lanham, MD: Rowman and Littlefield, 1998), pp. 21–60.

23 For general overviews of Turkey's Kurdish war, see David McDowall, *A Modern History of the Kurds,* pp. 418–444; Robert Olson (ed.), *The Kurdish Nationalist Movement in the 1990s: Its Impact on Turkey and the Middle East*; Kemal Kirisci and Gareth M. Winrow, *The Kurdish Question and Turkey: An Example of a Trans-State Ethnic Conflict*; Henri J Barkey and Graham E. Fuller, *Turkey's Kurdish Question.*

24 See, for example, Human Rights Watch, *'Still Critical'. Prospects in 2005 for Internally Displaced Kurds in Turkey,* March 2005, http://www.hrw.org/reports/2005/turkey0305/

25 Pam O'Toole, 'Europe's well-connected Kurds', http://news.bbc.co.uk/1/hi/world/europe/285102.stm

26 According to Soner Cagaptay and Ali Koknar, 'The PKK's new offensive: implications for Turkey, Iraqi Kurds, and the United States', *Policywatch,* no. 877, 25 June 2004, Washington Institute for Near East Policy, www.washingtoninstitute.org

27 For details on the KRG zone, see Tim Judah, 'In Iraqi Kurdistan', *Survival,* vol.44, no.4, winter 2002–03, pp. 38–51; Carole A. O'Leary, 'The Kurds of Iraq: recent history, future prospects', *MERIA,* vol. 6, no. 4, December 2002; Michiel Leezenberg,

'Economy and society in Iraqi Kurdistan: fragile institutions and enduring trends', in Toby Dodge and Steven Simon (eds), *Iraq at the Crossroads: state and society in the shadow of regime change*, Adelphi Paper no. 354 (Oxford: Oxford University Press for the IISS, January 2003), pp. 149–160; Gareth Stansfield, 'Continued developments threaten Iraq's territorial integrity', *Gulf News*, 18 May 2004. For a brief and critical appraisal of the KRG during the January 2005 elections, see Anna Ciezadlo, 'Kurds disgruntled with Kurdish parties', *New Republic*, 3 February 2005, reproduced in *Kurdistan Observer*, 4 February 2005.

[28] Peter W. Galbraith, 'As Iraqis celebrate, the Kurds hesitate', *New York Times*, 1 February 2005.

[29] For an account of the apparent contradictions in Turkish policy towards the KRG, see Philip Robins, *Suits and Uniforms: Turkish foreign policy since the Cold War* (London: Hurst and Co, 2003), pp. 312–342.

[30] Chris Kutschera, 'Iraqi Kurds agree to agree – for now', *The Middle East*, no. 329, December 2002, pp. 25–27; and, by the same author, 'Federalism first', *The Middle East*, no. 335, June 2003, pp. 20–21.

[31] See his 'Reflections on a sovereign Iraq', reproduced in the *Kurdistan Observer*, 8 February 2004.

[32] In an interview with Turkey's *TV Star*, reported in Cengiz Candar, 'Regime change in Iraq; repercussions for Turkey', July 2002, www.patrides.com/July02/enregime

[33] Bulent Aliriza, *CSIS Turkey Update*, 21 December 2001, www.csis.org.

[34] Reported in Cengiz Candar, 'Regime change in Iraq; repercussions for Turkey'.

[35] Reported in *ibid.*, and Bulent Aliriza, *CSIS Turkey Update*, 21 December 2001.

[36] For an analysis of the background and nature of the AKP see R. Quinn Mecham, 'From the ashes of virtue, a promise of light: the transformation of political Islam in Turkey', *Third World Quarterly*, vol. 25, no. 2, 2004, pp. 339–358.

[37] Quoted in *Turkish Daily News*, from the *Washington Post*, 'Washington Post: Turks would be a reluctant ally against Washington', 10 September 2002.

[38] Mark R. Parris, 'Starting over: US–Turkish relations in the post-Iraq era', *Turkish Policy Quarterly*, vol. 3, no. 1, spring 2003, http://www.turkishpolicy.com/

[39] The contents of the document were widely reported and discussed in the Turkish press. See Ertugrul Kurkcu, 'Washington pushed Turks toward "the red line"', MERIP Press Information Note 103, 6 August 2002, http://www.iraqwatch.org/perspectives/merip-pin103-080602.htm

[40] 'Turkey, US near accord on deployment', Karl Vick, *Washington Post*, 17 January 2003; 'Turks open borders to 20000 troops', *Daily Telegraph*, 28 January 2003. 'US prodding Turkey to be "more active"', *Turkish Daily News*, 3 February 2003; 'Ankara urged to back "military measures"', *Financial Times*, 3 February 2003. 'Americans in talks on Turkish troops', *International Herald Tribune*, 7 February 2003.

[41] 'Turkey plans thrust into Iraq to stop any Kurd war refugees', *International Herald Tribune*, 25 November 2002; and 'Turkey deploys troops near Iraqi border', 17 December 2002; 'Kurds deny US military buildup', 17 December 2002; 'General Staff denies reports of extraordinary build-up on Iraq border', 19 December 2002, all from *Turkish Daily News*.

[42] 'Americans in talks on Turkish troops', *International Herald Tribune*, 7 February 2003; 'US troop deal alarms Kurds', *The Guardian*, 10 February 2003; 'Explosive ingredients', *Guardian*, 13 February 2003; 'Turkey puts focus on future of Kurds', *Financial Times*, 24 February 2003; 'Kurds "terrified" at prospect of Turkish invasion', *The Independent*, 24 February 2003; 'Vote is nearing in Turkey on American use of bases', *International Herald Tribune*, 24 February 2003.

[43] 'US prodding Turkey to be "more active"', *Turkish Daily News*, 3 February 2003;

'Ankara urged to back "military measures"', *Financial Times*, 3 February 2003.

[44] 'Legal haggles snag deployment to Turkey' 9 February 2003; and 'Work can begin on bases', 10 February 2003, both *Washington Post*.

[45] 'Yakis, Babacan return from Washington talks', *Turkish Daily News*, 17 February 2003.

[46] Jon Gorvett, 'A hugely unpopular war', *The Middle East*, no. 328, November 2002.

[47] Article 92 of the Turkish constitution requires UN or NATO sanction for Turkey to engage in war, and Sezer interpreted the use of Turkish territory as a staging point as tantamount to Turkish involvement.

[48] The entire Republican Peoples Party (CHP) opposition – Kemalist, pro-TGS, and nationalistic – voted against.

[49] For a transcript of the interview, see http://www.defenselink.mil/transcripts/2003/tr20030506-depsecdef0156.html

[50] 'Wolfowitz remarks draw ire in Turkey', *Turkish Daily News,* 8 May 2003.

[51] For a general discussion of issues raised by Wolfowitz and of the Turkish response, see Nicole Pope, 'Wolfowitz's advice', *The Middle East*, no.700, 16 May 2003, pp. 23–24.

[52] As an example, see the interview given by Chief of the Turkish General Staff General Hilmi Ozkok, reproduced in full in *Turkish Probe*, 1 June 2003.

[53] Barak A. Salmoni, 'Strategic partners or estranged allies: Turkey, the United States, and Operation Iraqi Freedom', Strategic Insights vol. 2, no. 7, July 2003, http://www.ccc.nps.navy.mil/si/july03/middleeast.asp offers a good analysis of this debate.

[54] For accounts of this period, see Sabri Sayari 'Between allies and neighbours: Turkey's burden sharing policy in the Gulf conflict', in Andrew Bennett, Joseph Lepgold, and Danny Unger (eds), *Friends in Need: Burden Sharing in the Gulf War*, (London: Macmillan, 1997), pp.197–217; William Hale, 'Turkey, the Middle East, and the Gulf crisis', pp. 679–692.

[55] DoD News Briefing, Secretary of State Donald H. Rumsfeld and Gen. Myers, 21 March 2003, http://www.defense.gov/transcripts/2003/t03212003_t0321sd1.html

Chapter Two

[1] For a list of the membership of Iraq's interim government, and the text of the Transitional Administrative Law (TAL), see http://www.fco.gov.uk/Files/KFile/TAL,0.pdf

[2] TAL, Article 58(c).

[3] International Crisis Group, *Iraq: Allaying Turkey's fears over Kurdish ambitions*, Middle East Report no.35 (Ankara/Amman/Brussels: 26 January 2005), p. 3.

[4] For an account of the Kurdish role in the negotiations leading up to the TAL agreement, see International Crisis Group, *Iraq's Kurds: Toward an Historic Compromise?*, Middle East Report no.26, (Amman/Brussels: 8 April 2004), pp. 1–5.

[5] For example, 'Autonomy plan for Iraq Kurds worries Ankara', *Financial Times*, 12 March 2004.

[6] Steve Negus, 'Battling for Iraq's future', *Middle East International*, no. 716, 9 January 2004, pp. 4–7.

[7] The text of the letter is reproduced in www.kurdistanobserver.com

[8] See, for example, Aamer Madhani, 'Anti-American sentiment grows among Kurds', *Chicago Tribune*, reproduced in *Kurdistan Observer,* 15 June, 2004; and 'Barzani hints at secession', *Kurdistan Observer,* 29 June, 2004.

[9] 'Top Iraq cleric offers caution on UN Resolution', *Washington Post*, 7 June 2004.

[10] Numerous examples of Kurdish cooperation with coalition forces before, during, and after the March invasion are offered in Yossef Bodansky, *The Secret History of the Iraq War* (New York: Regan Books, 2004).

11 'US seeks to reassure Turkey over control of "Kurdish' cities", *Financial Times*; 'Kurdish victory provokes fears of Turkish invasion', *Independent;* 'Turkey told US will remove Kurd forces from city', *Guardian,* all 11 April 2003.

12 'Turkey eyes the Middle East: strategic realignments', *Strategic Comments*, vol.10, no.6, (London: International Institute for Strategic Studies, July 2004), www.iiss. org/stratcom

13 'Local council elected in Kirkuk, draws protests', *Turkish Daily News,* 26 May 2003.

14 'Iraqi Turkmen Front says US favours Kurds', *Turkish Daily News,* 5 June 2003; 'Turkmens call for power-sharing in administration of new Iraq', *Turkish Daily News,* 1 July 2003.

15 Edward Wong, '2 Kurdish parties close to forming unity government', *New York Times,* 20 December 2003.

16 'KDP, PUK to run jointly in January election', 2 December 2004, and 'Kurds close ranks in bid to secure federation from elected Iraqi assembly', 4 December 2004, both in *Kurdistan Observer.*

17 'Oil rich city will be major test for Iraq', *Washington Post*, 14 January 2004.

18 International Crisis Group, *Iraq's Kurds: Toward an Historic Compromise?*, Middle East Report no. 26 (Amman/Brussels: 8 April 2004) p.11.

19 See Human Rights Watch 16 (4E), *Reversing ethnic cleansing in Northern Iraq*, August 2004. This report offers a good account of Arabisation, Kurdish attempts to reverse it since April 2003, and the issues and difficulties this raises. For a Kurdish view, see Gareth Smyth, interview with Nechirvan Barzani, *Financial Times,* 28 January 2005, and reproduced in *Kurdistan Observer.*

20 International Crisis Group, *Iraq: allaying Turkey's fears over Kurdish ambitions*, Middle East Report No.35, (Ankara/ Amman/Brussels: 26 January 2005) p.3.

21 Human Rights Watch, *Reversing ethnic cleansing*, p. 48. See also International Crisis Group, *Iraq: allaying Turkey's fears*, pp. 2–3.

22 'Turkmen quit Kirkuk city council, say Kurds taking over', *Kurdistan Observer,* 28 March 2004.

23 Jackie Spinner, 'Ethnic groups try to stake claim on Kirkuk', *Washington Post,* 30 January 2005.

24 Nicholas Blanford, 'Some 200 Sadr militiamen March through Kirkuk', *Kurdistan Observer,* 8 March 2004; Michael Howard, 'Insurgents stir up strife in Kirkuk', *Washington Post*, 17 May 2004; and Gareth Stansfield, 'Continued developments threaten Iraq's territorial integrity', *Gulf News*, 18 May 2004.

25 International Crisis Group, *Iraq: allaying Turkey's fears*, p.5.

26 'New insurgency confronts US forces', 12 November 2004: 'Insurgents step up the battle for Mosul', 25 November 2004: and 'Mosul victim beheaded at roadside', 18 December 2004, all in the *Guardian.*

27 Michael Knights, 'Lessons from Mosul', Policywatch, no. 950, 27 January 2005. www.washingtoninstitute.org

28 Article 58a of the TAL commits the transitional government to 'act expeditiously to take measures to remedy the injustice caused by the previous regime's practices in altering the demographic character of certain regions, including Kirkuk', by restoring 'the (displaced) residents to their homes and property' and resettling those thereby displaced.

29 For details, see Human Rights Watch, *Reversing ethnic cleansing in Northern Iraq*, August 2004, pp. 55–77.

30 'Iraqi election creates unusual alliances', *Kurdistan Observer*, 30 November 2004. See also Kirsten Scharnberg, 'Leader warns Kurds must be allowed to re-establish majority in Kirkuk', *Chicago Tribune*, 10 December 2004.

31 'Kirkuk election deal tips power to Kurds, angers Arabs, Turkmen', 15 January 2005; 'Talabani: we have received assurances for Kirkuk', 23 January 2005, both *Kurdistan Observer.*

32 'An Arab party based in Kirkuk to boycott elections', *Kurdistan Observer,* 25 January 2005.

33   'PKK-linked parties to participate in Iraq elections', *Turkish Daily News,* 26 January 2005.

34   Selcan Hacaoglu, 'Turkey warns Kurds about Kirkuk control', *Kurdistan Observer,* and Yusuf Kanli, 'Turkey's Kirkuk anxiety', *Turkish Daily News,* both 27 January 2005.

35   'Kirkuk consensus', *Turkish Daily News,* 28 January 2005.

36   'Turkey appeals to UN for Kirkuk', *Turkish Daily News,* 25 January 2005.

37   Yusuf Kanli, 'Turkey won't sit back over Kirkuk spillover', *Turkish Daily News,* 28 January 2005.

38   'US policy on the status of Kirkuk', http://www.state.gov/r/pa/prs/ps/2005/40916.htm, 13 January 2005.

39   'Talabani: Kirkuk is Kurds' Jerusalem', *Turkish Daily News,* 31 December 2004.

40   Kirsten Scharnberg, 'Leader warns Kurds must be allowed to re-establish majority in Kirkuk', *Chicago Tribune,* 10 December 2004.

41   'Kurdish state is a "red line" for Syria, too', *Turkish Daily News,* 28 December 2004.

42   'Barzani sees Kirkuk joining southern Kurdistan', *Kurdistan Observer ,*18 October 2004.

43   'Iraqi Kurd leader warns neighbours not to meddle in Kirkuk issue', *Kurdistan Observer,* 17 October 2004.

44   'Massoud Barzani: Kurds ready to fight for Kirkuk', *Kurdistan Observer,* 13 October 2004.

45   'Kurdish leader: Kirkuk holds solution to future', 26 June 2004; and 'Barzani hints at secession', 30 June 2004, both *Kurdistan Observer.*

46   Gareth Smyth, Interview with Nechirvan Barzani, *Financial Times,* 28 January 2005.

47   International Crisis Group, *Iraq's Kurds,* p.7. This theme, that the Kurdish leadership in Iraq has hitherto exhibited a readiness to compromise that is neither understood nor supported by the Kurdish population generally, constitutes the main thrust of this report.

48   'Kurds lay ground for independence poll', *Daily Telegraph,* 9 January 2004, 'Iraqi Kurds seek referendum on a Kurdish state', *Kurdistan Observer,* 24 December 2004.

49   Kamil Mirawdeli, 'Voting for independence: people of Kurdistan make their choice', *Kurdistan Observer,* 8 February 2005.

50   Peter W. Galbraith, 'As Iraqis celebrate, the Kurds hesitate', *New York Times,* 1 February 2005.

51   Faik Bulut, 'Preparing the new Iraqi constitution – risk factor', *Turkish Daily News,* 8 February 2005.

52   For a general consideration of the role of Turkmen in Turkish foreign policy, see H.Tarik Oguzlu, 'The "Turkomans" as a Factor in Turkish Foreign Policy', *Turkish Studies,* vol.3, no.2, autumn 2002, pp.139–148.

53   For example, little support was offered to the many Turkmen who fell victim to Saddam's 'Arabisation'.

54   For an interesting comparison of British, Ottoman, and Iraqi figures for the demographic breakdown of 'Iraqi Kurdistan', see Nazhad Khasraw Hawramany, 'Ethnic distribution in Kirkuk, past and present', *Kurdistan Observer,* 15 January 2004.

55   'Turkmen quit Kirkuk city council, say Kurds taking over', *Kurdistan Observer,* 29 March 2004.

56   'If Kurds insist, Turkmen will demand a federal region', *Zaman* 5 January 2004.

57   Saadet Oruc, 'Iraqi Turcomans concerned about security', *Turkish Daily News,* 18 March 2002.

58   Middle East Programme Briefing Paper BP04/02, *Iraq in transition: vortex or catalyst?* (London: Chatham House, September 2004), p. 23.

59   International Crisis Group, I*raq: allaying Turkey's fears,* p. 10. See pp. 9-11 for a brief and useful summary of Ankara's relationship with the Turkmen of Iraq.

60   Yossef Bodansky, *The Secret History of the Iraq War* (New York: Regan Books, 2004), pp. 30-31.

61   Ilnur Cevik, 'Turkey flops on Iraqi Turkmens', *Turkish Probe,* reproduced in *Kurdistan Observer,* 23 March 2004.

62 Jean-Christophe Peuch, 'US–Turkey: Relations still racked by mutual distrust despite attempts to mend fences', www. rferl.org/features/2003/07/1707200316029

63 'Military outlines possible location for Iraq troops', *Turkish Daily News*, 27 September 2003.

64 Patrick Cockburn, 'Turks react with fury to massive US assault on northern city', *Independent*, 12 September 2004; Scheherezade Faramarzi, 'US allows Iraqis back to Tal Afar homes', *Washington Post*, 14 September 2004; 'US requests "warning" clarification', and 'Tal Afar turns to rubble', both *Turkish Daily News*, 15 September 2004; 'Turkey sending aid to Tal Afar in next few days', *Turkish Daily News*, 16 September 2004.

65 'Turkey, Iraq at odds over new border gate', *Turkish Daily News*, 12 March 2004; Mete Belovacikli, 'Tal Afar, Kirkuk, Mosul, Arbil, Tuz Khurmatu', *Turkish Daily News*, 15 September 2004.

66 Ilnur Cevik, 'Turkey flops on Iraqi Turkmens', *Turkish Probe*, reproduced in *Kurdistan Observer*, 23 March 2004.

67 'Kurds tell Ankara Arabisation true danger in Kirkuk', *Turkish Daily News*, 23 June 2004.

68 Ilnur Cevik, 'Start living in the real world in Iraq', *Turkish Daily News*, 26 May 2004.

69 'Kirkuk sensitivity', *Turkish Daily News*, 14 October 2004.

70 Kemal Kirisci, 'Between Europe and the Middle East: the transformation of Turkish policy', *MERIA*, vol.8, no.1, March 2004; and *Strategic Comments*, 'Turkey eyes the Middle East'.

71 Philip J. Robins, 'Avoiding the question', in Henri J. Barkey (ed), *Reluctant Neighbour: Turkey's role in the Middle East* (Washington DC: US Institute of Peace Press, 1996), pp. 179–203.

72 Mehmet Ali Burand, 'Is there a new role for Turkey in the Middle East?', in Henri J. Barkey, (ed), *Reluctant Neighbour: Turkey's role in the Middle East*, p. 171.

73 'PM says Turkey to pursue active foreign policy', *Turkish Daily News*, 5 January 2005.

74 A characterisation offered by Kemal Kirisci, 'Between Europe and the Middle East: the transformation of Turkish policy'

75 Soner Cagaptay, 'A Turkish rapprochement with Middle East rogue states?', *Policywatch*, no. 825, January 9 2004, Washington Institute of Near East Policy, p. 2, www.washingtoninstitute. org

76 Phebe Marr, 'Turkey and Iraq', in Henri J. Barkey, (ed), *Reluctant Neighbour: Turkey's role in the Middle East*, pp. 45–69.

77 'Ankara: "We will take Baghdad as a counterpart for the second border gate with Iraq, but not the Kurds"', *Turkish Daily News*, 19 June 2001.

78 See, for example, 'Ecevit: Saddam should allow arms inspectors to return', *Turkish Daily News*, 23 January 2002; and 'Ecevit warns Saddam: do not set the region on fire', *Turkish Daily News*, 11 February 2002.

79 'Turkish trade delegation urges Iraq to avert war', *Financial Times*, 10 January 2003.

80 'Turkey to drum up Arab support for war', *Financial Times*, 19 December 2002.

81 For a text of the communiqué, and for a report on the proceedings, see *Turkish Daily News*, 25 January 2003.

82 See the 14 February 2004 Kuwait address by Turkish Foreign Minister Abdullah Gul, http://www.mfa.gov. tr/MFA/PressInformation/Speeches/ Speeches2004/StatementByGul_ 14February2004.htm

83 Soner Cagaptay, 'A Turkish rapprochement with Middle East rogue states?', *Policywatch*, no. 825, 9 January 2004, Washington Institute of Near East Policy, p. 2, www.washingtoninstitute.org

84 'Kurds killed in Syria clashes', www. news.bbc.co.uk/1/hi/world/middle_ east/3517848, 16 March 2004; 'Syria urged to free riot Kurds', www.news.bbc. co.uk/1/hi/world/middle_east/3607059, 7 April 2004.

85 Gurgur Garrusi, 'Kurds riot in Iran', *Kurdistan Observer*, 11 March 2004.

86 Muhammad Muslih, 'Syria and Turkey: uneasy relations', in Henri J. Barkey, (ed), *Reluctant Neighbour: Turkey's role in the Middle East*, pp.113–129.

87 Quoted in Soner Cagaptay, 'A Turkish rapprochement with Middle East rogue states?'

88 See Gokhan Cetinsaya, 'Essential friends and natural enemies: the historic roots of Turkish–Iranian relations', *MERIA*, vol.7, no.3, September 2003; and Atila Eralp, 'Facing the challenge: post-revolutionary relations with Iran', Henri J. Barkey, (ed), *Reluctant Neighbour: Turkey's role in the Middle East*, pp.93–112.

89 'Iran reassures Turkey on border security', *Turkish Daily News*, 12 January 2004.

90 'Iran to declare Kongra-Gel as terrorist', *Turkish Daily News*, 21 July 2004.

91 'Erdogan says Iran visit not aimed against third countries', *Turkish Daily News*, 31 July 2004.

92 'Turkey denies shift in foreign policy', *Financial Times*, 8 April 2003. See also *Strategic Comments*, 'Turkey eyes the Middle East'.

93 See for example 'Syria and Iran aiding militants, Iraq says', *Guardian*, 20 February 2004.

94 'Malaysia urges Muslim peacekeeping force in Iraq under UN', *Washington Post*, 10 October 2003; 'Turkey faces tough task in getting OIC support for Iraq mission', *Turkish Daily News*, 13 October 2004; 'Turkey calls for Islamic peacekeeping call for Iraq', *Turkish Daily News*, 14 October 2004.

95 Seymour Hersh, 'Plan B', *New Yorker*, 28 June 2004.

96 See Soner Cagaptay, 'Kurds on the way to Turkey: how Israel can prevent a crisis in its relations with Turkey', *Ha'aretz*, 13 July 2004; Ed Blanche, 'Israel's alliance with Turkey', *Daily Star*, 17 July 2004; 'FM appears convinced by Israeli denial', *Turkish Daily News*, 23 June 2004.

97 See 'Rift in Kongra-Gel threatens return to violence', *Jane's Intelligence Review*, 1 June 2004. The following passage draws heavily on this report. As is common practice, the term PKK will continue to be used throughout to refer to Turkey's armed Kurdish opponents.

98 'PKK/KADEK claims to have disarmed', 6 January 2004; 'Osman Ocalan in Mosul', 23 June 2004; and 'Osman Ocalan: we have laid down our arms', 17 September 2004, all *Turkish Daily News*; 'The dispirited descent of Turkish rebel Kurds in Iraq', *Washington Post*, 26 September 2004. See also Michael Howard, 'In their Iraqi mountain hideaway Turkey's most wanted men stay loyal to their cause', *Guardian* 8 October 2003.

99 Ilnur Cevik, 'Who left the door open?', *Turkish Daily News*, 23 June 2004; Soner Cagaptay and Emrullah Eslu, 'Is the PKK still a threat to the United States and Turkey?', *Policywatch*, no. 940, 10 January 2005, Washington Institute for Near East Policy, www.washingtoninstitute.org

100 *Ibid.*

101 'Turkish army flexes muscles on Iraq, Cyprus', *Washington Post*, 16 January 2004.

102 'Gul: we will take care of PKK ourselves', in comments reported in the Turkish newspaper *Zaman* and reproduced in the *Kurdistan Observer*, 3 September 2004.

103 Reported in the *Kurdistan Observer*, 11 September 2004.

104 'Gul: US has lost the support of Turkish public', in comments reported in the Turkish newspaper *Zaman* and reproduced in the *Kurdistan Observer*, 24 November 2004.

105 *Jane's Intelligence Review* , 'Rift in Kongra-Gel'. See also Mehmet Ali Birand, 'PKK in northern Iraq not on the agenda anymore', *Turkish Daily News*, 5 May 2004.

106 For example, see 'US says no military action on PKK soon', *Turkish Daily News*, 19 June 2004.

107 'Remarks by Condoleeza Rice about Kurds in southern Kurdistan', *Kurdistan Observer*, 21 August 2004.

108 'Turkey loses patience with US stance on Kurdish rebels, PM warns', *Kurdistan Observer*, 4 September 2004.

[109] Reported in the *Kurdistan Observer*, 22 December 2004.

[110] 'Turkey presses Iraq on PKK extradition', *Turkish Daily News*, and 'US and Iraq agree on militants' return', *Zaman*, both 13 January 2005.

[111] 'Zaman asks, Edelman answers', *Zaman*, 10–11 January 2005.

[112] 'Priorities differ on PKK issue', *Turkish Daily News*, 12 January 2005.

[113] Soner Cagaptay, 'Time to shut down the PKK: why the US and Turkey should work together', *Policywatch*, no. 786, 12 September 2003, Washington Institute Near East Policy, www.washingtoninstitute.org

[114] 'Strains with America', *Newsweek*, 7 February 2005.

[115] Ambassador Nuzhet Kandemir (retired), in an interview with *Turkish Daily News*, 'The future of Iraq', 5 November 2005.

[116] See for example a *WorldNetDaily* report, 'Military calls for massive operation into Kurdish region', posted 12 November 2004, and reproduced in the *Kurdistan Observer*, 13 November 2004. The Turkish press also carried reports of the plans.

[117] Soner Cagaptay, 'Time to shut down the PKK: why the US and Turkey should work together', *Policywatch*; International Crisis Group, *Iraq: allaying Turkey's fears*, p.14.

[118] Details of Turkey's EU accession-related reform programme can be found at the Turkish Foreign Ministry website at www.mfa.gov.tr

[119] This point is made by Graham E. Fuller, 'Turkey's strategic model', *Washington Quarterly*, vol.27, no.3, summer 2004, pp.51–64.; and Mohammed Ayoob, 'Turkey's multiple paradoxes', *Orbis*, vol. 48, no. 3, summer 2004, pp. 451–463.

[120] See Ziya Onis, 'Domestic politics, international norms, and challenges to the state: Turkish–EU relations in the post-Helsinki era', *Turkish Studies*, vol.4, no.1, spring 2003, pp. 9–34.

[121] Regular report on Turkey's progress towards accession, http://europa.eu.int/comm/enlargement/turkey/index.htm

[122] See, for example, the statement issued on 12 December 2004 by a group of prominent Kurdish leaders associated with the Kurdish Institute of Paris, 'What do the Kurds want in Turkey?', found at www.kurdistanobserver.com See also, 'Kurds see bright future in EU', 9 October 2004; and 'Kurds ask Turkey for more democratic steps ahead of key EU summit', 4 December 2004, both *Kurdistan Observer*.

[123] 'Kurd activists set up new party', 23 October 2004; and 'Kurdish politicians lend support to Zana's call for new party', 4 November 2004, both *Kurdistan Observer*.

[124] Soner Cagaptay and Emrullah Eslu, 'Is the PKK still a threat to the United States and Turkey?'

[125] Dogu Ergil, 'Foreign policy challenges (2): Iraq', 7 February 2005; and Faik Bulut, 'Preparing the new Iraqi constitution; risk factor', 8 February 2005, both *Turkish Daily News*.

Chapter Three

[1] Quoted in Jackie Spinner, 'For proud minority, a "very happy day"', *Washington Post*, 31 January 2005.

[2] 'Kurds set to win two thirds of vote in Kirkuk', *Kurdistan Observer*, 2 February 2005.

[3] 'Talabani: Kirkuk is Kurds' Jerusalem', *Turkish Daily News*, 31 December 2004.

[4] 'Iraq in transition: vortex or catalyst?', Middle East Programme Briefing Paper 04/02, Chatham House, London, September 2004.

[5] *Ibid.*, p. 6. See also Dawn Brancati, 'Can federalism stabilise Iraq?', *Washington Quarterly*, vol. 27, no. 2, spring 2004, pp. 14–15 and 19–20 for a consideration of this possibility.

[6] 'Iraq in transition: vortex or catalyst?', p. 9.

[7.] *Ibid*, p. 16.

8   International Crisis Group, *Iraq's Kurds: Toward an Historic Compromise?*, Middle East Report no.26, (Amman/Brussels: 8 April 2004), p. i.

9   *Ibid.*

10   For some brief comment on the differences between the two leaders, see Gareth R.V. Stansfield, 'The Kurdish dilemma: the golden era threatened', in Toby Dodge and Steven Simon (eds), *Iraq at the crossroads: state and society in the shadow of regime change*, Adelphi Paper 354, (Oxford: Oxford University Press for the International Institute for Strategic Studies, 2003) pp. 131–147

11   For details of the KDP and PUK approach to 'de-Arabisation' since April 2003, see Human Rights Watch, *Reversing ethnic cleansing in Northern Iraq.*

12   Henry Kissinger, 'Reflections on a sovereign Iraq', reproduced in *Kurdistan Observer*, 8 February 2004

13   Nuzhet Kandemir, 'The future of Iraq', *Turkish Daily News*, 5 November 2004.

14   International Crisis Group, *Iraq: allaying Turkey's fears*, p. 12.

15   Comments made in an interview with Yusuf Kanli, 'Last minute warning: Turkey won't remain indifferent to sufferings of Turkmen', *Turkish Daily News*, 31 January 2005.

16   International Crisis Group, *Iraq: allaying Turkey's fears*, p. 12.

17   Kemal Kirisci, 'Between Europe and the Middle East: the transformation of Turkish policy'

18   'Iraq in transition: vortex or catalyst?', 'Iraq in transition', p.23.

19   'CIA sound alarm on Iraq civil war', *Kurdistan Observer*, 23 January 2004.

20   Christopher Catherwood, *Winston's Folly: Imperialism and the Creation of Modern Iraq* (London: Constable, 2004), p. 136.

21   *Ibid.*, p. 227.

22   Leslie H. Gelb, 'The three-state solution', *New York Times*, 25 November 2004. For the transcript of a debate with Martin Indyk on Gelb's arguments, held under the auspices of the Council for Foreign Relations, see www.cfr.org/publications.php?id=6749

23   Henry Kissinger, 'Reflections on a sovereign Iraq', reproduced in *Kurdistan Observer*, 8 February 2004.

24   *Ibid.*

25   See Peter Galbraith, 'How to get out of Iraq', *New York Review of Books*, 15 April 2004.

26   Doug Struck and Bassam Sebti, 'Iraq Shi'ite coalition tries to dispel fears of Iran-style rule', *Washington Post*, 16 January 2005.

27   Bradley Graham, 'US officials discount risk of Iran-style rule', *Washington Post*, 7 February 2005.

28   For comment, see *Strategic Comments*, vol. 10, no. 1, 'Iraq's constitution: breakthrough overshadowed by violence', March 2004, International Institute for Strategic Studies, London; 'Shi'ites balk at signing Iraqi interim constitution', *Washington Post*, 5 March 2004.

29   'Iraq in transition: vortex or catalyst?', p. 4.

30   This prospect is explored by Michael Gunter, 'The consequences of a failed Iraqi state: an independent Kurdish state in northern Iraq?', *Journal of South Asian and Middle Eastern Studies*, vol. 27, no. 3, spring 2004, pp. 1–11.

31   International Crisis Group, *Iraq: allaying Turkey's fears*, p. 15.

32   Michael Gunter, 'The consequences of a failed Iraqi state: an independent Kurdish state in northern Iraq?', *Journal of South Asian and Middle Eastern Studies*, vol. 27, no. 3, spring 2004, p.10.

33   Timothy Noah , 'Are the Kurds coming around?', *Kurdistan Observer*, 19 May 2004, reporting on an article by Hugh Pope and Bill Spindle, also on 19 May, in the *Wall Street Journal*.

34   'Bush and Clinton told Congress Saddam was smuggling oil', *Financial Times*, 19 January 2005.

35   See 'The Ankara-Erbil axis', reproduced in the *Kurdistan Observer* from the *National Review Online*, 2 February 2004; and 'Ilnur Cevik, 'New opening with the Iraqi Kurds?', *Turkish Daily News*, 16 February 2004.

36   Yusuf Kanli, 'Have we recognised the state of "Kurdistan?"' *Turkish Daily News*, 11 November 2004.

37 'Talabani: fight against PKK needs time', *Turkish Daily News*, 9 September 2004.

38 Ilnur Cevik, 'Iraqi Kurds courting Erdogan', 21 June 2004; and Cengiz Candar, 'Turkish–Kurdish rapprochement despite the Americans', 23 June 2004, both *Turkish Daily News*.

39 Ilnur Cevik, 'Ankara ponders new Iraq policy', *Turkish Daily News*, 10 November 2003.

40 'Kurds surprised by Turkey's stand on autonomy', *Turkish Daily News*, 28 June 2004.

41 International Crisis Group, *Iraq: allaying Turkey's fears*, p. 16.

42 *Ibid.*

43 For a recent examples of this from the Turkish side, see 'US ties above everything, says Gul', *Turkish Daily News* 4 January 2005.

44 During an interview with Larry King, at www.dod.mil/transcripts/2005/tr20050203-secdef2084

45 Ian O. Lesser, 'Turkey in the EU: a new US relationship', *Insight Turkey*, vol. 6, no. 4, October–December 2004, p. 36.

46 For details of Turkish public opinion and how it compares globally see the chapter entitled 'Global opinion: the spread of anti-Americanism', in the Pew Research Centre's Trends 2005, http://pewresearch. org/trends/trends2005-global.pdf

47 'US says no plan to station more F-16s at Incirlik', *Turkish Daily News*, 2 February 2005. For more information on the Review see Statement by Douglas J. Feith, Undersecretary of Defense for policy, before the House Armed Services Committee, 23 June 2004, www.defenselink.mil/policy/speech/june_23_04.html

48 'Feith seeks anti-nuke cooperation, reassures over Kirkuk', *Turkish Daily News*, 1 February 2005.

49 Deputy Secretary Paul Wolfowitz interview with CNN TURK, http://www.dod.mil/transcripts/2004/tr20040129-depsecdef0382.html

50 For comment on the Bush administration's Middle East Initiative, see Philip H. Gordon, 'Bush's Middle East vision', *Survival*, vol. 45, no. 1, spring 2003, pp. 155–165.

51 This point is made by Graham E. Fuller, 'Turkey's strategic model; myths and realities', *The Washington Quarterly*, vol. 27, no. 3, summer 2004, pp. 51–64, and by Mohammed Ayoob, 'Turkey's multiple paradoxes', *Orbis*, vol. 48, no. 3, summer 2004, pp. 451–463.

52 Abdullah Gul, 'Turkey's role in a changing Middle East environment', *Mediterranean Quarterly*, vol. 15, no. 1, winter 2004, p.7.

53 www.mfa.gov.tr/grupa/ai/islamicconference.1.htm

54 http://www.mfa.gov.tr/MFA/Ministry/TheMinister/SpeechesofMinister/Statement_AbdullahGul_Thirty-FirstSessionIslamicConferenceForeignMinisters_Istanbul_14+June+2004

55 'Gul says Mideast drive no matter of "prestige"', *Turkish Daily News*, 5 January 2005.

56 'PM says Turkey to pursue active foreign policy', *Turkish Daily News*, 5 January 2005.

57 'US sees Turkey can play positive role in Mideast process', *Turkish Daily News*, 5 January 2005.

58 www.whitehouse.gov/news/releases/2004/06/20040629.4.html

59 Abdullah Gul, 'Turkey's role in a changing Middle East environment', p.5.

60 For a strong statement of this line of thinking by two senior US figures, see Morton Abramowitz and Richard Burt, 'High stakes for Turkey and the west', *Washington Post*, 20 August 2004.

61 See Ziya Onis, 'Domestic politics, international norms, and challenges to the state: Turkish-EU relations in the post-Helsinki era', pp. 9–34.

62 Regular Report on Turkey's progress towards accession. www.europa.eu.int/comm/enlargement/report_2004/

63 Graham E. Fuller, 'Turkey's strategic model', *Washington Quarterly*, vol. 27, no.3, summer 2004, p. 63.

ADELPHI PAPERS

The Adelphi Papers monograph series is the Institute's flagship contribution to policy-relevant, original academic research.

Eight Adelphi Papers are published each year. They are designed to provide rigorous analysis of strategic and defence topics that will prove useful to politicians and diplomats, as well as academic researchers, foreign-affairs analysts, defence commentators and journalists.

From the very first paper, Alastair Buchan's 'Evolution of NATO' (1961), through Kenneth Waltz's classic 'The Spread of Nuclear Weapons: More May Be Better' (1981), to influential additions to the series such as Mats Berdal's 'Disarmament and Demobilisation after Civil Wars' (1996) and Lawrence Freedman's 'The Revolution in Strategic Affairs' (1998), Adelphi Papers have provided detailed, nuanced analysis of key security issues, serving to inform opinion, stimulate debate and challenge conventional thinking. The series includes both thematic studies and papers on specific national and regional security problems. Since 2003, Adelphi Paper topics have included 'Strategic Implications of HIV/AIDS', 'Protecting Critical Infrastructures Against Cyber-Attack', 'The Future of Africa: A New Order in Sight', 'Human Rights and Counter-terrorism in America's Asia Policy', 'Somalia: State Collapse and the Threat of Terrorism', 'Counter-terrorism: Containment and Beyond', 'Japan's Re-emergence as a "Normal" Military Power', and 'Weapons of Mass Destruction and International Order'.

Longer than journal articles but shorter than books, Adelphi Papers permit the IISS both to remain responsive to emerging strategic issues and to contribute significantly to debate on strategic affairs and the development of policy. While the format of Adelphi Papers has evolved over the years, through their authoritative substance and persuasive arguments recent issues have maintained the tradition of the series.

RECENT **ADELPHI PAPERS** INCLUDE:

Adelphi Paper 372
Iraq's Future:
The aftermath of regime change
Toby Dodge
ISBN 0-415-36389-6

Adelphi Paper 373
Fuelling War:
Natural resources and armed conflict
Philippe Le Billon
ISBN 0-415-37970-9